400
Questions & Answers
ABOUT THE
BOOK OF MORMON

SUSAN EASTON BLACK

Covenant Communications Inc

Cover image *Mormon Abridging the Plates* by Tom Lovell © Intellectual Reserve, Inc.

Cover design copyrighted 2011 by Covenant Communications, Inc.

Published by Covenant Communications, Inc.
American Fork, Utah

Printed in China
First Printing: October 2011
20 19 18 17 16 15 14 13 12 11   10 9 8 7 6 5 4 3 2 1

ISBN 978-1-60861-390-8

Introduction

When I was ten years old, memorable adventures in the classroom were rare. Any variety in the daily routine of school doldrums was welcomed. Recess, assemblies, and lunch time provided some relief, but nothing came close to "religious released time": two weeks in which fifth- and sixth-grade students didn't attend school. For two weeks these students attended a local church to study religion and received school credit for so doing. It seems odd today that such was the case in a public school setting in California's Long Beach School District in the 1950s, but so it was. A note requiring the signature of a parent to attend "religious released time" was all that was needed for what I viewed as a "school vacation."

My father refused to sign the much-needed note. He would not allow me to attend religious services at a local Catholic cathedral, Jewish synagogue, or nondenominational church to learn about religion. After all, my father was an LDS bishop. He was visibly upset that the Mormon Church was not on the list of approved churches to attend. It didn't occur to him that there were not any other Mormons in my class. I tried to console myself that school wouldn't be that bad, but for two weeks while my friends attended religious classes, I attended school alone. Can you imagine how boring a classroom can be with no friends and precious little diversion?

The following year I vowed would be better for me. I would attend "religious released time"! Running errands at home and cleaning my room all had the qualifying string, "Now will you let me attend 'religious released time'?" I took every opportunity to remind my father of the personal disaster school had been without friends.

The night before "religious released time" was to begin in sixth grade, my father finally gave in and agreed that I could go each day to the nondenominational church if I wore my green felt Primary bandalo and carried a large-size Book of Mormon. In retrospect I can only suppose my father assumed that I would be fully clad in the armor of God and ready for any assault to my budding testimony.

The attack came that first day from the minister of the non-denominational church. As he spoke to the assembled children, he said, "Children, God is in a cloud. God is in a tree. God is in a flower and in a raindrop." How was this possible? I knew that God had a body. If God was in a raindrop, which drop? Without much forethought or respect, I jumped to my feet and yelled, "Stop!"

The minister stopped. The boys and girls, who had been whispering and passing notes, stopped. Everyone stared as I said, "What you have just said is not true!"

"What is not true?" the minister asked as wide-eyed classmates looked on.

"God does not live in a cloud, a tree, a flower, or a raindrop," I said. "God has a body."

Visibly upset, the minister asked, "How do you know that?"

I quickly looked at my Primary bandalo, hoping it would give me a clue about the source of my knowledge. I saw plastic musical notes, a seagull, and scroll. I then looked to the book I was holding. I held up the Book of Mormon and said, "It says so in this book."

"Oh, that," replied the minister. He cut short the opening devotional in the chapel and invited the other children to attend their religious classes for the day. He invited me to come to his office.

A large circle of friends pointed the way to the minister's office, but I alone entered his room. He inquired about my bandalo, but he was much more interested in my book. "Where in that book does it say God has a body?" he asked.

I flipped through the pages quickly, hoping to open to just the right verse.

"You appear to be having difficulty locating what you are seeking. Could it be that you have never read the Book of Mormon?" he asked.

I admitted, "I have never read the book."

A sense of embarrassment led me to read the Book of Mormon. In all honesty, I cannot say that I had an experience equal to Parley P. Pratt's first reading of the sacred text. "I read all day," wrote Parley. "Eating was a burden, I had no desire for food; sleep was a burden when the night came, I preferred reading to sleep. As I read, the spirit of the Lord was upon me, and I knew and comprehended that the book was true, as plainly and manifestly as a man comprehends and knows that he exists. My joy was now full" (*Autobiography of Parley P. Pratt*, 36–37). Yet I can say that I read intently looking for any reference to God having a body.

I was disappointed not to find the answer in the beginning of 1 Nephi. As I read on, I learned about travels in the wilderness, broken bows, dreams, wickedness, and warfare. I found the Book of Mormon contained many messages, yet my first reading left me in a quandary. Where was the answer I was seeking? I did not find it. It was not until years later that I discovered the answer.[1] That answer and more are contained in *400 Questions and Answers about the Book of Mormon*. It is my hope that readers will find their questions answered in this book and that their testimonies of the truthfulness of the Book of Mormon will be strengthened.

I express gratitude to my colleagues at Brigham Young University for sharing with me many ideas and insights about the Book of Mormon, especially scholars Todd Compton and David Seely. Their example of scholarship and faithful devotion to truth blesses my life and that of countless students. I am very appreciative of my fine research assistants—Clinton Brimhall, Sarah Allen, Chanel Arts, and Rebecca Allen—for sharing their many talents with me. And to my husband, Harvey, I express heartfelt admiration for his consistent example of righteous living. He exemplifies to me all that is good.

The Coming Forth of the Book of Mormon

"There is not a man or woman that loves the truth,
who has heard the report of the Book of Mormon,
but the Spirit of the Almighty has testified to him or her of its truth;
neither has any man heard the name of Joseph Smith,
but the Spirit has whispered to him—'He is a true Prophet.'"

—*Brigham Young*[2]

What is the importance of Joseph Smith's role as translator of the Book of Mormon?

Joseph Smith was the seer chosen "to bring forth my word . . . and not to the bringing forth my word only, saith the Lord, but to the convincing them of my word, which shall have already gone forth among them" (2 Ne. 3:11). Joseph was prepared—not by man, but by the Lord to be the translator of "another testament of Jesus Christ." Joseph is known to Latter-day Saints as "a seer, a

Joseph Smith

translator, a prophet, an apostle of Jesus Christ, an elder of the church through the will of God the Father, and the grace of [the] Lord Jesus Christ" (D&C 21:1). Through the instrumentality of Joseph Smith, Nephi's intent in writing—"that I may persuade men to come unto the God of Abraham, and the God of Isaac, and the God of Jacob, and be saved"— is now a reality. People throughout the world have access to the words of Nephi and other prophetic scribes due to the inspired translation of Joseph Smith (see 1 Ne. 6:4). The "difficulty of engraving . . . words upon plates" (Jacob 4:1) has proven fruitful, and the purposes of the Lord have been fulfilled as the word of God has "come forth unto the Gentiles, by the gift and power of the Lamb" through the instrumentality of Joseph Smith (1 Ne. 13:35). The very fact that the Book of Mormon exists is a testament that Joseph was the translator of ancient records.

When did Joseph Smith first learn that he would be an instrument in the hands of God in bringing forth the Book of Mormon?

On Sunday evening, September 21, 1823, in Manchester, New York, young Joseph Smith supplicated the Lord "for forgiveness of all my sins and follies, and also for a manifestation to me, that I might know of my state and standing before him" (JS–H 1:29). While calling on the Lord, Joseph said, "I discovered a light appearing in my room, which continued to increase until the room was lighter than at noonday, when immediately a personage appeared at my bedside, standing in the air, for his feet did not touch the floor" (JS–H 1:30). The angelic being "called [Joseph] by name, and said unto me that he was a messenger sent from the presence of God to me, and that his name was Moroni" (JS–H 1:33). The messenger told Joseph that "God had a work for me to do; and that my name should be had for good and evil among all nations, kindreds, and tongues, or that it should be both good and evil spoken of among all people" (JS–H 1:33). The conflicting reputation would center on a book written on gold plates and a Urim and Thummim prepared "for the purpose of translating the book" (JS–H 1:35). As the angel conversed with Joseph, "the place where the plates were deposited"

The Smith cabin in Manchester, New York

was shown him in vision (JS–H 1:42). When the vision closed, "the room was again left dark" and Joseph was left alone with his thoughts (JS–H 1:43). Before dawn, the messenger appeared two more times to converse with the seventeen-year-old youth. The angelic visitation of September 21, 1823, is the most detailed description of an angelic appearance in all of holy writ.[3]

Was it the angel Moroni or Nephi who visited Joseph Smith on the evening of September 21, 1823?

Joseph Smith was clear when he said that the angelic personage "called me by name, and said unto me that he was a messenger sent from the presence of God to me, and that his name was Moroni" (JS–H 1:33).

On April 15, 1842, the *Times and Seasons*—an LDS newspaper published in Nauvoo, Illinois—referred to the angel who visited Joseph Smith in September 1823 as "Nephi." The "Nephi" reference was perpetuated in another LDS newspaper, the *Millennial Star,* which was published in England. In an attempt to correct the erroneous assumption that the angel was named Nephi, Elder Orson Pratt wrote, "To John Christensen, Dear Bro.—Yours of the 9th inst. is rec'd. You inquire whether it was the Angel Nephi or Moroni who visited the Prophet on the night of the 21st and the 22nd Sept. 1823? As Moroni holds the keys of the stick or Record of Ephraim we have reason to believe that Moroni was that angel. This discrepancy in the history to which you refer may have occurred through the ignorance or carelessness of the historian or transcriber."[4]

Moroni, son of Mormon, was the last writer of the Book of Mormon. Moroni saw Jesus Christ (see Ether 12:39) and was ministered to by the three Nephite disciples (see Morm. 8:11). Moroni was entrusted with the records of two civilizations— the Nephites and the Jaredites. Following the battle at Cumorah, he wandered alone for many years in the Americas.[5]

When the angel Moroni visited Joseph Smith in 1823, he quoted from the words of Isaiah, Malachi, and Joel. Did he quote from any other Old Testament prophets?

The Pearl of Great Price account of the angelic visit to Joseph Smith in 1823 does not state that Moroni quoted the words of Jeremiah. However, in April 1835 Oliver Cowdery, the main scribe to the Book of Mormon translation, published in the LDS newspaper *Messenger and Advocate* that Jeremiah 16:16 was also quoted by Moroni to the young Joseph Smith and that Jeremiah's prophecy was soon to be fulfilled.[6] The prophecy in Jeremiah 16:16 states, "Behold, I will send for many fishers, saith the Lord, and they shall fish them; and after will I send for many hunters, and they shall hunt them from every mountain, and from every hill, and out of the holes of the rocks."

Who was the first to know that the angel Moroni visited young Joseph Smith on September 21, 1823?

On September 22, 1823, the day following Moroni's first visitation, Joseph Smith walked from the family log home in Manchester, New York, to the family farm and began the "necessary labors of the day" (JS–H 1:48). In so doing, he discovered

The Smith farm in Manchester, New York

"my strength so exhausted as to render me entirely unable" to assist in harvesting the fields (JS–H 1:48). While in the act of returning home, he was again visited by the angel Moroni, who "related unto me all that he had related to me the previous night, and commanded me to go to my father and tell him of the vision and commandments which I had received" (JS–H 1:49).

In obedience to the angelic directive, Joseph returned to the family farm and told his father about the things that had transpired. Father Smith assured his young son of the divine nature of the visitations by saying, "It was of God" (JS–H 1:50). Joseph then went directly to the hill he had seen in vision the night before, "a hill of considerable size, and the most elevated of any in the neighborhood," about three miles southeast of the Smith farm

(JS–H 1:51). There, "under a stone of considerable size, lay the plates, deposited in a stone box" (JS–H 1:51). Joseph's attempt to take the plates out of the box was "forbidden by the messenger" (JS–H 1:53). Joseph was told that "the time for bringing them forth had not yet arrived" (JS–H 1:53).[7]

Why was Joseph Smith prevented from obtaining the gold plates in 1823?

Oliver Cowdery wrote that as Joseph Smith started toward the hill "a thought would start across his mind on the prospects of obtaining so desirable a treasure— one in all human probability sufficient to raise him above a level with the common earthly fortunes of his fellow men, and relieve his family from want, in which, by misfortune and sickness they were placed." Oliver continued, "It is sufficient to say that such were his reflections during his walk of from two to three miles: the distance from his father's house to the place pointed out. And to use his own words it seemed as though two invisible powers were influencing, or striving to influence his mind—one with the reflection that if he obtained the object of his pursuit, it would be through the mercy and condescension of the Lord, and the other with the tho'ts [thoughts] and reflections like those previously mentioned—contrasting his former and present circumstances in life with those to come."[8] Moroni had cautioned Joseph in September 1823 "that Satan would try to tempt me (in consequence of the indigent circumstances of my father's family), to get the plates for the purpose of getting rich. This he forbade me, saying that I must have no other object in view in getting the plates but to glorify God" (JS–H 1:46).

Did the Smiths believe that young Joseph conversed with an angel?

The Smiths accepted Joseph's account of the angel Moroni's visitations. They accepted his description of "the ancient inhabitants of this continent, their dress, mode of traveling, and the animals upon which they rode, their cities, their buildings, with every particular; their mode of warfare; and also their religious worship." Mother Lucy Mack Smith wrote of her son's description of early

American inhabitants by saying, "This he would do with as much ease, seemingly, as if he had spent his whole life with them." She added, "I presume our family presented an aspect as singular as any that ever lived upon the face of the earth, all seated in a circle, father, mother, sons and daughters, and giving the most profound attention to a boy." The Smiths had implicit confidence in young Joseph. "Truly ours was a happy family," wrote Mother Smith, "although persecuted by the preachers, who declared there was no more vision, the canon of scripture was full, and no more revelation was needed."[9]

On what other occasions besides the annual visits on the hill did the angel Moroni converse with Joseph Smith?

Lucy Mack Smith recorded a visit of the angel Moroni with Joseph Smith that occurred outside the annual visits. She told of Joseph returning home one evening later than expected in the spring of 1827. When his father asked about his lateness, "Presently [Joseph] smiled, and said in a calm tone, 'I have taken the severest chastisement that I have ever had in my life.'" Father Smith was "quite angry" with what he assumed was the action of some man in town. Joseph replied, "Stop, father, stop . . . it was the angel of the Lord: as I passed by the hill of Cumorah, where the plates are, the angel met me, and said that I had not been engaged enough in the work of the Lord; that the time had come for the Record to be brought forth; and that I must be up and doing, and set myself about the things which God had commanded me to do."[10]

> Other than the Smith family, who was privileged to learn that Joseph had seen an angel and knew the whereabouts of gold plates?

Martin Harris, known as "an industrious, hardworking farmer, shrewd in his business calculations, frugal in his habits, and what was termed a prosperous man in the world," was the first outside the Smith family to know that Joseph Smith had seen gold plates. Martin learned about Joseph Smith and gold plates while building a spacious one-and-a-half-story frame house. The anticipated building project was expansive and beyond the grasp of less fortunate citizens in Palmyra, but not Martin Harris. He wanted his house to be a showplace and every detail of its construction was well attended. The beautiful farmhouse was nearly finished by 1824. Only a few details remained—rocking up a well on the east side of the kitchen entrance and walling up the basement. To complete the minor tasks, Martin employed laborers—Joseph Smith Sr. and his son Hyrum. "Each day while they were there, Martin would find excuse to bring up the

Martin Harris

matter" of young Joseph Smith and rumors surrounding his visions "and would ask many questions, referring frequently to the Bible to prove that heavenly messengers visiting the earth was not a new doctrine. Finally, during the course of their conversations, Mr. Smith took Martin into his confidence. . . . Martin was thrilled beyond expression. He requested that he be kept posted on any new developments."[11]

> **How many years passed between Joseph Smith's first visitation from the angel Moroni and his acquiring the gold plates and the Urim and Thummim?**

Four years passed between Joseph Smith's first visitation with the angel Moroni and his receipt of the plates and the Urim and Thummim. During those years (1823–1827), the Smiths listened as Joseph spoke of heavenly truths. Family members expressed implicit confidence in his vision and his knowledge concerning the plates. When his brother William was asked, "Did you not doubt Joseph's testimony sometimes?" he replied, "No we all had the most implicit confidence in what

he said. He was a truthful boy. Father and mother believed him, why should not the children? . . . we never doubted his word for one minute."[12]

> **Why did Joseph Smith charge his family not to mention heavenly truths outside the family circle?**

Joseph Smith explained to his family, "The world was so wicked that when they came to a knowledge of these things they would try to take our lives." Promise as they might to keep it quiet, news of angelic visitations and preparations to receive the gold plates spread to the community of Palmyra. "False reports, misrepresentations, and base slanders, flew as if upon the wings of the wind in every direction." Neighbors strained to hear fanciful accounts then retorted with mockery and ridicule. Yet the Smiths remained calm. They were "now confirmed in the opinion that God was about to bring to light something upon which we could stay our minds, or that would give us a more perfect knowledge of the plan of salvation and the redemption of the human family."[13]

The night Joseph received the gold plates

When did Joseph Smith receive the gold plates?

Near midnight on September 22, 1827, Joseph climbed the hill where the plates were deposited and there was met by the angel Moroni, who "delivered [the gold plates] up to me with this charge: that I should be responsible for them; that if I should let them go carelessly, or through any neglect of mine, I should be cut off; but that if I would use all my endeavors to preserve them, until he, the messenger, should call for them, they should be protected" (JS–H 1:59).

In what ways did Joseph Smith physically protect the ancient plates?

As word of gold treasure spread from house to house in Palmyra, assailants tried to take what they called "Joe's Gold Bible." Cash and property were offered for a glimpse of the plates. When Joseph Smith refused, schemes were contrived to snatch the treasure. Keeping the plates safe proved difficult for Joseph. A birch log, hearth stones, floorboards, flax, and a barrel of beans were variously used to hide the plates. Joseph later wrote,

"Several times I was shot at, and very narrowly escaped, and every device was made use of to get the plates away from me."[14]

What shape were the rings that bound the plates?

The plates were bound together into a single volume by three rings. As to the shape of the rings, John Whitmer—one of the Eight Witnesses who saw the plates—wrote, "Each [ring was] in the shape of a D with the straight line towards the centre."[15]

Box thought to store the gold plates when they were not being hidden

Of the many persecutions that Joseph Smith faced in Palmyra, which was the most publicized?

It would appear that that the most publicized persecution was a lawsuit. Lucy Harris, wife of Martin Harris, entered a "complaint against Joseph, before a certain magistrate of Lyons, [New York]," charging him

Replica of the gold plates

with never having "the Record which he professed to have, and that he pretended to have in his possession certain gold plates, for the express purpose of obtaining money." In March 1829 charges against Joseph Smith were heard in the court at Lyons, New York. In the ensuing case, Martin Harris testified, "I can swear that Joseph Smith never has got one dollar from me by persuasion, since God made me. I did once, of my own free will and accord, put fifty dollars into his hands, in the presence of many witnesses, for the purpose of doing the work of the Lord. This, I can pointedly prove; and I can tell you, furthermore, that I have never seen in Joseph Smith, a disposition to take any man's money without giving him a reasonable compensation for the same in return. And as to the plates which he professes to have, gentlemen, if you do not believe it, but continue to resist the truth, it will one day be the means of damning your souls." The magistrate wasted no time in announcing that it would not be necessary to call other witnesses. He ordered the court clerk to bring him "what had been written of the testimony already given. This he tore in pieces before their eyes, and told them to go home about their business, and trouble him no more with such ridiculous folly."[16]

Who was the first scribe of the Book of Mormon translation?

Martin Harris was the first scribe. He wrote as Joseph translated the book of Lehi, the first abridged book inscribed on the gold plates. The writing and translation process took place in the east end of an upstairs room of the Joseph Smith Jr. farmhouse in Harmony, Pennsylvania. According to Martin Harris, "a thick curtain or blanket was suspended" from the ceiling in the room in which Joseph translated the book of Lehi. Once Joseph "concealed [himself] behind the blanket," he looked "through his spectacles, or transparent stones" to read the inscriptions. As he read aloud, each word was "written down by [Martin], who sat on the other side of the suspended blanket."[17]

How did Martin Harris get permission to take the 116-page manuscript translation of the book of Lehi to Palmyra?

On more than one occasion, Martin Harris expressed reservations about the veracity of the work in which he and Joseph Smith were engaged. Hoping to free himself of doubt, he asked Joseph if he could see the plates. His request was denied. The denial did not stop Martin from importuning Joseph about the matter or asking for "liberty to carry the writings home and show them" to his wife Lucy and other family members. Joseph said, "[He] desired of me that I would inquire of the Lord, through the Urim and Thummim, if he might not do so. I did inquire, and the answer was that he must not."

Martin was disappointed, but continued as scribe while Joseph dictated during the months of April and May 1828. Yet he still struggled with doubts. He wanted tangible evidence of the gold plates. He again broached the subject with Joseph. This time he asked for permission to take the scribed manuscript to Palmyra. This was again denied. When he returned to Harmony his thoughts were of asking Joseph a third time for the manuscript.[18] When Martin asked a third time, he was granted permission to take the 116-page manuscript to Palmyra.

Who was allowed to see the 116 manuscript pages that Martin Harris took to Palmyra?

"Permission was [given Martin] to have the writings on certain conditions; which were, that he show them only to his brother, Preserved Harris, his own wife, his father and his mother [Nathan and Rhoda Harris], and a Mrs. Cobb [Polly Harris Cobb], a sister to his wife." Martin agreed to the specified conditions. He entered into a written covenant with Joseph Smith "in a most solemn manner that he would not do otherwise than had been directed" and required of him.

Martin then "took the writings, and went his way" on June 14, 1828, about two months after the translation of the book of Lehi had begun.[19]

How long was the book of Lehi manuscript in Martin Harris's possession?

Martin had the manuscript in his possession for three weeks—until about July 7, 1828. At first, Martin was most circumspect in showing the manuscript only to the named family members. But Martin soon showed the manuscript to anyone who called at his home—or, as Joseph Smith wrote, "Notwithstanding . . . the great restrictions which he had been laid under, and the solemnity of the covenant which he had made with me, he did show them to others."[20]

How did Joseph Smith learn that the book of Lehi manuscript was missing?

When Martin Harris "had been absent nearly three weeks, and Joseph had received no intelligence whatever from him, which was altogether aside of the arrangement when they separated," Joseph Smith journeyed to Palmyra from Harmony, Pennsylvania, to see Martin and re-

Joseph at Emma's sickbed while anxiously waiting for Martin Harris to return with the 116-page manuscript

cover the manuscript. Mother Smith reported that as soon as Joseph arrived at her farmhouse, he requested that Martin be sent for at once. Anticipating a quick response, victuals were set on the table at 8 AM. The Smiths "waited till nine, and [Martin] came not—till ten, and he was not there—till eleven, still he did not make his appearance." It was not until "half-past twelve" that Martin was seen "walking with a slow and measured tread towards the house, his eyes fixed thoughtfully upon the ground." When he reached the gate in the yard,

"he stopped, instead of passing through, and got upon the fence, and sat there some time with his hat drawn over his eyes."

When Martin entered the house, he sat down at the table next to those who were already seated. "He took up his knife and fork as if he were going to use them, but immediately dropped them." Seeing this, Hyrum Smith asked, "Martin, why do you not eat; are you sick?" He pressed "his hands upon his temples" and cried with "a tone of deep anguish, 'Oh, I have lost my soul! I have lost my soul!'" Joseph, who was seated at the table, jumped to his feet and asked, "Martin, have you lost that manuscript? have you broken your oath, and brought down condemnation upon my head, as well as your own?"

"Yes, it is gone," replied Martin, "and I know not where."

"Oh, my God!" said Joseph "All is lost! all is lost! What shall I do? I have sinned—it is I who tempted the wrath of God. I should have been satisfied with the first answer which I received from the Lord; for he told me that it was not safe to let the writing go out of my possession." He wept and paced the floor in agony."21

In what way was Martin Harris rebuked for the lost manuscript?

Martin's rebuke was felt on two fronts—temporal and spiritual. The temporal rebuke happened the very day he confessed to Joseph Smith about the lost manuscript. Lucy Mack Smith believed it no coincidence that "a dense fog spread itself over his fields, and blighted his wheat while in the blow, so that he lost about two-thirds

of his crop, whilst those fields which lay only on the opposite side of the road received no injury whatever." The spiritual rebuke came by revelation in July 1828: "When thou [Joseph] deliveredst up that which God had given thee sight and power to translate, thou deliveredst up that which was sacred into the hands of a wicked man [Martin Harris], Who has set at naught the counsels of God, and has broken the most sacred promises which were made before God" (D&C 3:12–13).22

What was Joseph's share or part in the Lord's displeasure over the lost manuscript?

Although Martin Harris lost the manuscript, Joseph Smith was also responsible. Joseph's rebuke was swift—he lost the right to translate the gold plates. The Urim and Thummim was taken from him, and a severe chastisement was pronounced by the Lord (see D&C 3).

After a time, Joseph received the plates and Urim and Thummim and began again to translate the ancient record. How did he describe the translation process?

On November 13, 1843, Joseph Smith wrote to James Arlington Bennett and explained the translation process: "By the power of God I translated the Book of Mormon from hieroglyphics; the knowledge of which was lost to the world; in which wonderful event I stood alone, an unlearned youth, to combat the worldly wisdom, and multiplied ignorance of eighteen centuries, with a new revelation; which, (if they would receive the everlasting Gospel,) would open the eyes of [the world], and make 'plain the old paths,' wherein if a man walk in all the ordinances of God blameless, he shall inherit eternal life."[23]

What details did scribes of the Book of Mormon add about the translation process?

During the translation process, scribe David Whitmer observed, "Joseph Smith would put the seer stone into a hat, and put his face in the hat, drawing [the hat] closely around his face to exclude the light; and in the darkness the spiritual light would shine. A piece of something resembling parchment would appear, and on that appeared the writing. One character at a time would appear, and under it was the interpretation in English. Brother Joseph would read off the English to Oliver Cowdery, who was his principal scribe, and when it was written down and repeated to Brother Joseph to see if it was correct, then it would disappear, and another character with the interpretation would appear."[24]

How did Emma Smith describe the translation process?

In an 1856 interview Emma Smith recalled, "When my husband was translating the Book of Mormon, I wrote a part of it, as he dictated each sentence, word for word, and when he came to proper names he could not pronounce, or long words, he spelled them out, and while I was writing them, if I made any mistake in spelling, he would stop me and correct my spelling, although it was impossible for him to see how I was writing them down at the time."

Later, in an 1879 interview, Emma said that Joseph "would dictate to me hour after hour; and when returning after meals, or after interruptions, he could at once begin where he had left off, without either seeing the manuscript or having any portion of it read to him. This was a usual thing for him to do. It would have

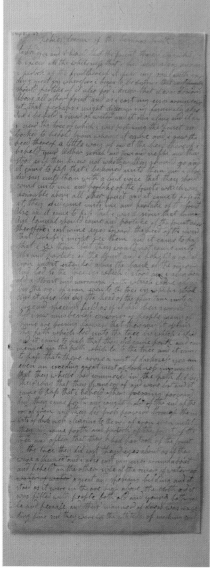

Original Manuscript of the Book of Mormon

been improbable that a learned man could do this; and, for one so ignorant and unlearned as he was, it was simply impossible."

In the same interview, she also stated, "I frequently wrote day after day, often sitting at the table close by him, he sitting with his face buried in his hat, with the stone in it, and dictating hour after hour with nothing between us. . . . The plates often lay on the table without any attempt at concealment, wrapped in a small linen tablecloth, which I had given him to fold them in. I once felt of the plates, as they thus lay on the table, tracing their outline and shape. They seemed to be pliable like thick paper, and would rustle with a metallic sound when the edges were moved by the thumb, as one does sometimes thumb the edges of a book."[25]

How do modern Book of Mormon scholars feel about the description of the translation process given by David Whitmer and Emma Smith?

Royal Skousen, a professor of English language at Brigham Young University, weighed in on the translation process and the question of whether Joseph Smith spelled proper names. Skousen writes, "Over the twenty-one years that I have worked on [the Book of Mormon Manuscript Project] . . . We now know much more about the original text of the Book of Mormon, especially its Hebrew-like syntax, archaic vocabulary, and systematic phraseology. And we now have a much clearer insight into how Joseph Smith translated (however one interprets the word *translate*), with strong evidence that he dictated the text word for word and that he controlled for the spelling of the strange Book of Mormon names."[26] Although Skousen's arguments are very strong, Brant Gardner, a writer and speaker on the Book of Mormon and expert on Mesoamerican studies, reasons that the translation was to a large extent an idea and that Joseph Smith had some liberty to state things in his own idiom or to borrow the language of the King James Version of the Bible.

What portion of the Book of Mormon did Joseph Smith scribe?

According to Royal Skousen,

Joseph Smith "acted as scribe for 28 words of the original manuscript."[27] These are in Alma 45:22, which reads, "Therefore, Helaman and his brethren went forth to establish the church again in all the land, yea, in every city throughout all the land which was possessed by the people of Nephi. And it came to pass that they did appoint priests and teachers throughout all the land, and over all the churches."

The principal scribe for the Book of Mormon translation was Oliver Cowdery. What did Oliver say of the translation process?

Oliver Cowdery testified, "I wrote with my own pen the entire book of mormon (Save a few pages) as it fell from the Lips of the prophet [Joseph Smith]. As he translated [it] by the gift and power of god, By [the] means of the urum and thummim, or as it is called by that book holy Interpreters. I beheld with my eyes. And handled with my hands the gold plates from which it was translated. I also beheld the Interpreters. That book is true. Sidney Rigdon did not write it. Mr [Solomon] Spaulding did not write it. I wrote it myself as it fell from the Lips of the prophet. It contains the everlasting Gospel, to preach to every nation, kindred, tongue and people. It contains principles of Salvation, and if you my hearers, will walk by its light, and obey its precepts, you will be saved with an everlasting salvation in the Kingdom of God."[28]

What is contained in the sealed portion of the gold plates?

Oliver Cowdery said that the sealed portion "contains the same revelation which was given to John upon the isle of Patmos, and when the people of the Lord are prepared, and found worthy, then it will be unfolded unto them."[29] As to what portion of the plates was sealed, there is not conclusive evidence. Book of Mormon scholar H. Donl Peterson estimated that "if one third was sealed—and we presently have a publication containing 531 pages—then the Book of Mormon would eventually contain approximately 797 pages. . . . If two-thirds of the Book of Mormon was sealed, then the entire record, when published, will contain about 1,593 pages."[30]

What circumstance led to Oliver Cowdery, David Whitmer, and Martin Harris becoming the Three Witnesses of the Book of Mormon?

Oliver Cowdery, David Whitmer, and Martin Harris asked Joseph Smith to "inquire of the Lord" and ask if they might be privileged to be witnesses of the gold plates. Joseph said, "They became so very solicitous, and urged me so much to inquire that at length I complied, and through the Urim and Thummim" received an answer: "The testimony of three of my servants . . . shall go forth with my words" (D&C 5:11).[31]

In a nearby wooded area just beyond the Peter Whitmer Sr. home in Fayette, New York, Joseph, Oliver, David, and Martin tried to "obtain, by fervent and humble prayer, the fulfilment of the promises given"—that of viewing the plates. After kneeling down, "according to previous arrangement," Joseph prayed aloud to God. He was followed "by each of the others in succession," yet they did not receive a "manifestation of divine favor." Believing it still possible, they "again observed the same

The Three Witnesses

and showed them the plates. There were now two witnesses of the Book of Mormon, but what of the third?

Joseph left David and Oliver and went in search of Martin. He found him "at a considerable distance, fervently engaged in prayer." Martin told Joseph that "he had not yet prevailed with the Lord, and earnestly requested me to join him in prayer, that he also might realize the same blessings which we had just received." Joseph and Martin knelt together in supplication to God. "The same vision was opened to our view, at least it was again opened to me," Joseph wrote, "and I once more beheld and heard the same things; whilst at the same moment, Martin Harris cried out, apparently in an ecstasy of joy, ''Tis enough; 'tis enough; mine eyes have beheld; mine eyes have beheld;' and jumping up, he shouted, 'Hosanna,' blessing God, and otherwise rejoiced exceedingly."[32]

order of prayer, each calling on and praying fervently to God in rotation." The result was as before.

After the second failure, Martin "proposed that he should withdraw himself from us, believing, as he expressed himself, that his presence was the cause of our not obtaining what we wished for." Accordingly, he walked away. In his absence, the three remaining men "knelt down again, and had not been many minutes engaged in prayer" when an angel appeared

Where did the Eight Witnesses of the Book of Mormon see the gold plates?

Eight other men were shown the plates near the Joseph Smith

Sr. log home in Manchester, New York, "where the [Smith] family were in the habit of offering up their secret devotions to God." A written testimony that is published in the Book of Mormon was prepared by these eight men—Christian Whitmer, Jacob Whitmer, Peter Whitmer Jr., John Whitmer, Hiram Page, Joseph Smith Sr., Hyrum Smith, and Samuel H. Smith.[33] "The difference between the testimony given the Three Witnesses and that given to the Eight, is that the former was attended by a splendid display of the glory and power of God and the ministration of an angel, while the latter was attended by no such display, but was a plain, matter-of-fact exhibition of the plates by the Prophet to his friends; and they not only saw the plates, but handled them and examined the engravings upon them."[34]

Joseph and the Eight Witnesses

In what section of the Book of Mormon was the testimony of the witnesses first published?

The testimony of the Three Witnesses and the Eight Witnesses appeared at the end of the first edition of the Book of Mormon. Their testimony has followed the title page in all subsequent editions of the book.[35]

What circumstances suggest that Mary Whitmer, mother of four of the Eight Witnesses and mother-in-law of one, saw the gold plates and an angel?

Joseph Smith completed the translation of the Book of Mormon in the Peter Whitmer home. According to historical accounts, Mary Whitmer felt burdened by the additional guests. It is claimed at that time Mary saw the gold plates and an angel. John C. Whitmer, grandson of Mary Whitmer, claimed that he heard his grandmother relate the following: "She met a stranger carrying something on his back that looked like a knapsack. At first she was a little afraid of him, but when he spoke to her in a kind, friendly tone and he began to explain to her the nature of the work which was going on in her house, [translation of the final pages of the Book of Mormon] she was filled with inexpressible joy and satisfaction. He then untied his knapsack and showed her a bundle of plates, which in size and appearance corresponded with the description subsequently given by the witnesses to the Book of Mormon. This strange person turned the leaves of the book of plates over, leaf after leaf, and also showed her the engravings upon them; after which he told her to be patient and faithful in bearing her burden."[36] There are no writings of Mary Whitmer to verify or deny this account.

When did Joseph Smith return the plates to the angel Moroni?

Joseph Smith did not specify a particular date or place for returning the plates. He did not mention going with Oliver Cowdery to the Hill Cumorah. Joseph wrote, "According to arrangements, the messenger called for them [and] I delivered them up to him; and he has them in his charge until this day" (JS–H 1:60).

On June 17, 1877, at a stake conference held in Farmington,

Utah, Brigham Young said, "When Joseph got the Plates, the angel instructed him to carry them back to the Hill Cumorah, which he did. Oliver Cowdery says that when Joseph and he went there, the hill opened, and they walked into a cave, in which there was a large and spacious room. He says that he did not think, at the time, whether they had the light of the sun or artificial light, but it was as light as day. They laid the Plates on a table. It was a large table that stood in the middle of the room. Under this table there was a pile of plates as much as two feet high, and there were altogether in this room more plates than many wagon loads. They were piled up in the corners and along the walls. The first time they went there, the Sword of Laban hung upon the wall, but when they went again, it had been taken down and laid upon the table across the Gold Plates. It was unsheathed, and on it was written these words, 'This Sword will never be sheathed again until the kingdoms of this world become the Kingdom of our God and His Christ.' I tell you this as coming not only from Oliver Cowdery, but others who were familiar with it, and who understood it just as well as we understand coming to this meeting enjoying the day, and by and by we separate and go away, forgetting most of what is said, but remembering some things. So it is with other circumstances in life. I relate this to you, and I want you to understand it. I take this liberty of referring to those things so that they will not be forgotten and lost."[37]

What became of the original manuscript of the Book of Mormon?

The original manuscript as dictated by Joseph Smith to scribes was placed in the cornerstone of the Nauvoo House in the 1840s. In 1882 Lewis Bidamon, second husband of Emma Smith, removed the manuscript from the cornerstone. Upon doing so, he discovered that the manuscript was damaged by mold and water. Over the next six years, Lewis Bidamon gave away fragments and large pieces of the manuscript. According to Royal Skousen, "Only 28 percent of the original manuscript is extant, including a large number of fragments."[38]

Where is the printer's manuscript of the Book of Mormon located? What is its condition?

The printer's manuscript, written between August 1829 and March 1830, is fully extant except the first leaf is missing three lines. The printer's manuscript was copied from the original manuscript by Oliver Cowdery, Hyrum Smith, and an unknown scribe and was used in the publication of the first edition of the Book of Mormon. By 1850 the printer's manuscript was in the possession of David Whitmer. In 1888 David Whitmer's grandson George Schweich received possession of the manuscript. In 1903 George Schweich sold the printer's manuscript to the Reorganized Church of Jesus Christ of Latter Day Saints (Community of Christ). The manuscript remains with the Community of Christ. [39]

What difficulties were associated with finding a printer for the Book of Mormon?

Joseph Smith negotiated with Egbert B. Grandin—a Palmyra printer, bookseller, and publisher of the *Wayne Sentinel*—to print the Book of Mormon manuscript. Grandin declined, "believing the whole affair to be a wicked imposture and a scheme to defraud Mr. [Martin] Harris."

Room in the Grandin Building where the Book of Mormon was typeset

Grandin Building, where the Book of Mormon was printed

The response was the same when Joseph met with Thurlow Weed, former publisher of the *Rochester Daily Telegraph* and then editor of the Rochester *Anti-Masonic Enquirer.* Joseph and Martin Harris then called on Elihu F. Marshall, a book publisher in Rochester, New York. He agreed to publish the manuscript, but at an exorbitant price.

It was then that Joseph asked Martin Harris to financially secure the publication. Martin considered his request and accepted the financial burden of the publication cost. With his acceptance sure, Joseph and Martin approached publisher E. B. Grandin again, hoping that he would reconsider publishing the Book of Mormon. Grandin took "the advice of several discrete, fair-minded neighbors" who assured him that his connection with the book would be nothing more than a business matter. Their advice and Martin's willingness to enter a contractual agreement led Grandin to agree to publish the manuscript.[40]

What was Martin Harris's contractual agreement with E. B. Grandin?

On August 25, 1829, Martin entered into a mortgage agreement with Grandin guaranteeing that before the expiration of eighteen months from the August 1829 date, he would pay the requisite $3,000 to cover the publication costs. In case of nonpayment of monies, the sale of his acreage (about 150 acres) would cover the cost of printing.[41]

How prompt was Martin Harris in paying his debt to publisher E. B. Grandin?

It was not until April 1, 1831—twenty months after entering the contractual agreement with Egbert B. Grandin—that Martin Harris agreed to sell to Thomas Lakey 150 acres for $20 per acre on April 1, 1831. The deed or indenture for the requisite acres was signed by Martin Harris and Thomas Lakey at Lyons, New York, on April 7, 1831.[42]

What type of press was used for printing the Book of Mormon?

The Book of Mormon was printed on a Smith Patented Improved Press manufactured by Robert Hoe & Company of New York City. In 1906 President Joseph F. Smith purchased the exact press used to print the Book of Mormon. Today the press is on permanent exhibit at the Museum of Church History and Art in Salt Lake City.[43]

What events caused the printing of the Book of Mormon to be slower than expected?

Printing of some 296,000 pages of text was slow. One reason for the slow process was that additional type ordered for the job did not arrive from Albany, New York, until late November 1829. Other reasons were based on rumors suggesting that Martin Harris would not sell his mortgaged acreage or pay the full cost of printing. Grandin was concerned.

Adding to Grandin's growing fears, citizens of Palmyra passed a resolution calling on all residents to boycott any purchase of the Book of Mormon and to use their influence to prevent others from buying the book.

Several Palmyra townsfolk called on Grandin to express their opposition. Grandin was persuaded by their arguments

The room where the Book of Mormon was printed

and suspended printing of the Book of Mormon in January 1830.[44]

> What led E. B. Grandin to proceed with publication of the Book of Mormon within days of stopping the press?

On January 16, 1830, Martin Harris and Joseph Smith reached an agreement to sell the Book of Mormon until sufficient copies had been sold to pay the publishing costs. The agreement was as follows: "I hereby agree that Martin Harris shall have an equal privilege with me & my friends of selling the Book of Mormon of the Edition now printing by Egbert B Grandin until enough of them shall be sold to pay for the printing of the same or until such times as the said Grandin shall be paid for the printing the aforesaid Books or copies. Joseph Smith Jr, Manchester January the 16th 1830, Witness, Oliver H P Cowdery."[45] With the agreement in place, Grandin resumed printing the Book of Mormon.

When was the Book of Mormon available for sale by E. B. Grandin?

Convinced that Martin Harris would make good on their contractual agreement, a relieved Egbert B. Grandin announced on March 19, 1830, through the Palmyra newspaper the *Wayne Sentinel*, "The 'Book of Mormon' will be ready for sale in the course of next week." On March 26, 1830, he advertised, "First Public Sale of the Book of Mormon: the above work, containing about 600 pages, large Deuodecimo, is now for sale, wholesale and retail, at the Palmyra Bookstore, by E. B. Grandin."[46] The price of the Book of Mormon was equivalent to a two-day wage of an adult laborer. The price ranged from $1.25 to $1.75 per book.[47]

Who received the first copy of the Book of Mormon?

Martin Harris gave the first copy of the Book of Mormon to his brother Emer Harris on March 26, 1830, the very day the publisher announced that the book was for sale. That copy is now housed in the Church History Library in Salt Lake City.[48]

Why wasn't Joseph Smith present at the Grandin bookstore when the first copies of the Book of Mormon were released for public sale?

Joseph Smith was not in the Palmyra vicinity when the first copies of the Book of Mormon were released for sale. In late March 1830 as Joseph Smith approached Palmyra, he was surprised to find Martin Harris crossing the road ahead with "a Bunch of morman Books." Martin greeted Joseph by saying, "'The Book will not sell for no Body wants them.' Joseph says, 'I think they will sell well.'"[49]

How did members of Joseph Smith's family feel about the veracity of the Book of Mormon?

Joseph Smith's family immediately recognized the truthfulness of the Book of Mormon. For example, his mother, Lucy Mack Smith, did not hesitate to proclaim the power of the Book of Mormon and her son's role in translating the word of God. According to Mother Smith, after she was introduced to Mr. Ruggles, a Presbyterian pastor, the pastor remarked, "And you are the mother of that poor, foolish, silly boy, Joe Smith, who pretended to translate the Book of Mormon."

Lucy replied, "I am, sir, the mother of Joseph Smith; but why do you apply to him such epithets as those?"

The pastor retorted, "Because that he should imagine he was going to break down all other churches with that simple 'Mormon' book."

"Did you ever read that book?" Lucy inquired.

"No," said he, "it is beneath my notice."

"But," rejoined Lucy, "The Scriptures say, 'prove all things'; and, now, sir, let me tell you boldly, that that book contains the everlasting gospel, and it was written for the salvation of your soul, by the gift and power of the Holy Ghost."

"Pooh," said the minister. "Nonsense—I am not afraid of any member of my church being led astray by such stuff; they have too much intelligence."

"Now, Mr. Ruggles," said Lucy. "Mark my words—as true as God lives, before three years we will have more than one-third of your church; and, sir, whether you believe it or not, we will take the very deacon, too."

The minister responded to Lucy's vow with a hearty laugh. Soon after, Elder Jared Carter was called to preach in the minister's vicinity. Lucy wrote, "[Elder Carter] went immediately into the midst of Mr. Ruggles' church, and, in a short time, brought away seventy of his best members, among whom was the deacon [Samuel Bent], just as I told the minister."[50]

On another occasion Deacon Beckwith said to Lucy, "Mrs. Smith, you and the most of your children have belonged to our church for some length of time, and we respect you very highly. You say a good deal about the Book of Mormon. . . . I wish, that if you do believe those things, you would not say anything more upon the subject."

Recognizing his calculated rebuke, Lucy declared her right to speak of the Book of Mormon: "'Deacon Beckwith,' said I, 'if you should stick my flesh full of faggots, and even burn me at the stake, I would declare, as long as God should give me breath, that Joseph has got that Record, and that I know it to be true.'"[51]

"When the book of Mormon was first printed, it came to my hands in two or three weeks afterwards," recalled Brigham Young. "I examined the matter studiously for two years before I made up my mind to receive that book. I knew it was true, as well as I knew that I could see with my eyes, or feel by the touch of my fingers, or be sensible of the demonstration of any sense. Had not this been the case, I never would have embraced it to this day."[52]

Wilford Woodruff said, "The spirit bore witness that the record which [the Book of Mormon] contained was true. I opened my eyes to see, my ears to hear, and my heart to understand. I also opened my doors to entertain the servants of God."[53]

Ezra Taft Benson added, "The Book of Mormon is the instrument that God designed to 'sweep the earth as with a flood, to gather out [His] elect' (Moses 7:62). This sacred volume of scripture needs to become more central in our preaching, our teaching, and our missionary work. . . . We need to read daily from the pages of the book that will get a man 'nearer to God by abiding by its precepts, than by any other book.'"[54]

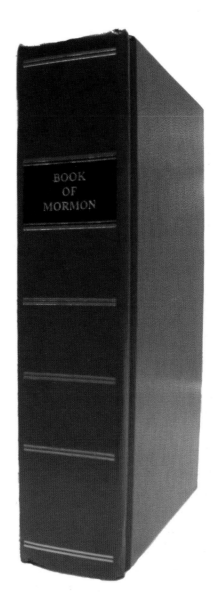

Replica of the first edition of the Book of Mormon

What did Joseph Smith say about the Book of Mormon?

From his youth in Palmyra to his manhood in Nauvoo, Joseph Smith testified of the origin and contents of the Book of Mormon. Joseph Smith never modified, mitigated, nor varied from his earliest pronouncement that God had called him to translate an ancient record that contained the fulness of the gospel.

In a priesthood meeting held in Kirtland, Ohio, Joseph likened the Book of Mormon to a mustard seed: "Take the Book of Mormon. . . . Like the mustard seed, [it] becomes the greatest of all herbs. And it is truth, and it has sprouted and come forth out of the earth, and righteousness begins to look down from heaven, and God is sending down His powers, gifts and angels, to lodge in the branches thereof."[55]

On Sunday, November 28, 1841, Joseph spent the day in council with the Quorum of the Twelve Apostles at the home of Brigham Young in Nauvoo, Illinois. He spoke with them about the scriptural message of the Book of Mormon: "I told the brethren that the Book of Mormon was the most correct of any book on earth, and the keystone of our religion, and a man would get nearer to God by abiding by its precepts, than by any other book."[56] Joseph's statement underscores his testimony that the Book of Mormon provides strength central to the restored gospel of Christ. [57]

Joseph also said, "Take away the Book of Mormon, and the Revelations, and where is our religion? We have none; for without a Zion, and a place of deliverance, we must fall; because the time is near when the sun will be darkened, and the moon turn to blood, and the stars fall from heaven, and the earth reel to and fro. Then, if this is the case, and if we are not sanctified and gathered to the places where God has appointed, with all our former professions and our great love for the Bible, we must fall; we cannot stand; we cannot be saved; for God will gather His Saints out from the Gentiles, and then comes desolation or destruction, and none can escape, except the pure in heart who are gathered."[58]

Joseph Smith

2

The Book of Mormon Is Another Testament of Jesus Christ

"And we talk of Christ, we rejoice in Christ, we preach of Christ, we prophesy of Christ, and we write according to our prophecies, that our children may know to what source they may look for a remission of their sins."

(2 Ne. 25:26)

How is the Book of Mormon another testament of Jesus Christ?

The divinity of Jesus Christ is powerfully proclaimed by prophets in the Old and New Testaments and in the Book of Mormon. The Book of Mormon record, kept by an ancient people living from 600 BC to AD 421, has come forth as a powerful second witness of Christ. From the time that Lehi left the land of Jerusalem in 600 BC until Moroni deposited the plates in the Hill Cumorah in AD 421, this account remained in the possession of Lehi and his posterity. Prophets from this lineage wrote of their

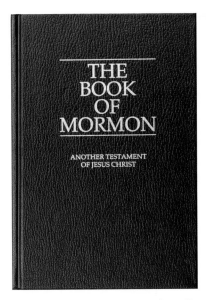

The Book of Mormon: Another Testament of Jesus Christ

knowledge, faith, and testimony of the Beloved Son of God. Through their faithful efforts and through divine intervention, the promised stick of Joseph—known in latter days as the Book of Mormon—has come forth as prophesied by Ezekiel: "Behold, I will take the stick of Joseph [the Book of Mormon], which is in the hand of Ephraim, and the tribes of Israel his fellows, and will put them with him, even with the stick of Judah [the Bible], and make them one stick, and they shall be one in mine hand" (Ezek. 37:19). The Book of Mormon and the Holy Bible are witnesses of the divine mission of Jesus Christ. These sacred records speak of the divinity of the Son of God, His ministry, and His holy teachings.

What evidence suggests that Jesus Christ is the focal point of the Book of Mormon?

Book of Mormon prophetic scribes primarily testified about Jesus Christ. As they wrote their testimonies of the Beloved Son of God, they mentioned some form of His name on an average of every 1.7 verses. The prophetic scribes referred to Jesus Christ by literally 101 different names

from the first reference to Him as "Lord" in 1 Nephi 1:1 to His final name in the Book of Mormon—"Eternal Judge," given in Moroni 10:34. Each of the 101 names signifies a different attribute or characteristic of Jesus. Each name is used appropriately to convey recognition of who Jesus is and what His mission represents.

How does the number of name references to Jesus Christ in the New Testament compare to the number in the Book of Mormon?

Book of Mormon prophetic scribes use some term referring to Christ on an average of once every 1.7 verses; in the New Testament, He is referred to on an average of once every 2.1 verses.[59] Thus, references to the Savior appear more frequently in the Book of Mormon than in the New Testament. Realizing that a verse of scripture typically consists of one sentence, on average readers of the Book of Mormon cannot read two sentences without seeing some term or name referring to Christ.

How are name references for Christ distributed throughout the Book of Mormon?

BOOKS	REFERENCES TO CHRIST	VERSES	AVERAGE
1 Nephi	474	618	1.303
2 Nephi	591	779	1.318
Jacob	156	203	1.301
Enos	22	27	1.227
Jarom	8	15	1.875
Omni	20	30	1.500
Words of Mormon	15	18	1.200
Mosiah	492	785	1.596
Alma	1,013	1,975	1.950
Helaman	225	497	2.209
3 Nephi	293	788	2.689
4 Nephi	42	49	1.167
Mormon	188	227	1.207
Ether	220	433	1.968
Moroni	163	166	1.028
TOTALS	3,925	6,607	1.7

Name references for Jesus Christ are not distributed equally throughout the text. For example, fewer references to Christ are present during periods of apostasy, military/political intrigue, or war (such as Alma 50–59). During periods of peace and prosperity, when the Nephites were keeping the commandments of God and listening to the words of holy prophets, names for Christ are profuse (see 4 Nephi).

By what names is Jesus Christ known in the Book of Mormon?

Listed alphabetically are the names for Jesus Christ in the Book of Mormon. The Book of Mormon reference next to the name shows one verse in which the name/reference appears.

Almighty (2 Ne. 23:6)

Almighty God (Jacob 2:10)

Alpha and Omega (3 Ne. 9:18)

Being (Mosiah 4:19)

Beloved (2 Ne. 31:15)

Beloved Son (2 Ne. 31:11)

Christ (2 Ne. 10:3)

Christ Jesus (Alma 5:44)

Christ the Son (Alma 11:44)

Counselor (2 Ne. 19:6)

Creator (2 Ne. 9:5)

Eternal Father (Mosiah 15:4)

Eternal God (1 Ne. 12:18)

Eternal Head (Hel. 13:38)

Eternal Judge (Moro. 10:34)

Everlasting Father (2 Ne. 19:6)

Everlasting God (1 Ne. 15:15)

Father (Jacob 7:22)

Father of Heaven (1 Ne. 22:9)

Father of Heaven and of Earth (Hel. 14:12)

Founder of Peace (Mosiah 15:18)

God (2 Ne. 1:22)

God of Abraham (1 Ne. 19:10)

God of Abraham, and Isaac, and Jacob (Mosiah 7:19)

God of Abraham, and of Isaac, and the God of Jacob (1 Ne. 19:10)

God of Isaac (Alma 29:11)

God of Israel (1 Ne. 19:7)

God of Jacob (2 Ne. 12:3)

God of Miracles (2 Ne. 27:23)

God of Nature (1 Ne. 19:12)

God of the Whole Earth (3 Ne. 11:14)

Good Shepherd (Alma 5:38)

Great Creator (2 Ne. 9:5)

Great Spirit (Alma 18:2)

Head (Jacob 4:17)

Holy Child (Moro. 8:3)

Holy God (2 Ne. 9:39)

Holy Messiah (2 Ne. 2:6)

Holy One (2 Ne. 2:10)

Holy One of Israel (1 Ne. 19:14)

Holy One of Jacob (2 Ne. 27:34)

Husband (3 Ne. 22:5)

Immanuel (2 Ne. 18:8)

Jehovah (Moro. 10:34)

Jesus (2 Ne. 31:10)

Jesus Christ (2 Ne. 25:19)

Keeper of the Gate (2 Ne. 9:41)

King (2 Ne. 16:5)

King of Heaven (2 Ne. 10:14)

Lamb (1 Ne. 13:35)

Lamb of God (1 Ne. 10:10)

Lord (1 Ne. 10:14)

Lord God (2 Ne. 1:5)

Lord God Almighty (2 Ne. 9:46)

Lord God of Hosts (2 Ne. 13:15)

Lord God Omnipotent (Mosiah 3:21)

Lord Jehovah (2 Ne. 22:2)

Lord Jesus (Moro. 6:6)

Lord Jesus Christ (Mosiah 3:12)

Lord of Hosts (1 Ne. 20:2)

Lord of the Vineyard (Jacob 5:8)

Lord Omnipotent (Mosiah 3:5)

Maker (2 Ne. 9:40)

Man (3 Ne. 11:8)

Master (Jacob 5:4)

Mediator (2 Ne. 2:28)

Messiah (1 Ne. 1:19)

Mighty God (2 Ne. 6:17)

Mighty One of Israel (1 Ne. 22:12)

Mighty One of Jacob (1 Ne. 21:26)

Most High (2 Ne. 24:14)

Most High God (Alma 26:14)

Only Begotten of the Father (2 Ne. 25:12)

Only Begotten Son (Jacob 4:5)

Prince of Peace (2 Ne. 19:6)

Prophet (1 Ne. 22:20)

Rabbanah (Alma 18:13)

Redeemer (1 Ne. 10:6)

Redeemer of Israel (1 Ne. 21:7)

Redeemer of the World (1 Ne. 10:5)

Rock (1 Ne. 15:15)

Savior (2 Ne. 31:13)

Savior Jesus Christ (3 Ne. 5:20)

Savior of the World (1 Ne. 10:4)

Shepherd (1 Ne. 13:41)

Son (2 Ne. 31:13)

Son of God (1 Ne. 10:17)

Son of Righteousness (Ether 9:22)

Son of the Eternal Father (1 Ne. 11:21)

Son of the Everlasting God (1 Ne. 11:32)

Son of the Living God (2 Ne. 31:16)

Son of the Most High God (1 Ne. 11:6)

Stone (Jacob 4:16)

Supreme Being (Alma 11:22)

Supreme Creator (Alma 30:44)

True and Living God (1 Ne. 17:30)

True Messiah (2 Ne. 1:10)

True Shepherd (Hel. 15:13)

True Vine (1 Ne. 15:15)

Well Beloved (Hel. 5:47)

Wonderful (2 Ne. 19:6)

What are the attributes of Jesus Christ revealed in the 101 names or references?

Each of the names or titles signifies a different attribute or characteristic of Jesus Christ.

For example:

Almighty God signifies a holy being having all power and unlimited might.

Alpha and Omega, the first and last letters of the Greek alphabet, refers to the timelessness and eternal nature of God.

Beloved Son signifies Christ's beloved status and His divine Sonship to the Father.

Counselor bears record of His preeminent position among men where judgment and prudence are needed.

Creator refers to the creations of God, for as the Apostle Paul wrote, "For by him were all things created, that are in heaven, and that are in earth" (Col. 1:16).

Eternal God signifies that God is from everlasting to everlasting, beyond finite comprehension in power, dominion, godly attributes, and eternal glory.

God of Israel announces His covenant relationship with Israel.

God of Nature proclaims that all things in nature are created, upheld, governed, and controlled by Him.

Holy Messiah signifies His holy state and His position as the promised, anointed Deliverer and King.

Holy One of Israel refers to Christ being the embodiment of holiness and the God of Israel, who came into the world through the lineage of that chosen people.

Jehovah (YHWH) is the name by which God is known to Israel.

Keeper of the Gate means that Christ opens the gate of salvation to the righteous and bars the gate to the wicked.

King signifies that He rules over the heavens and the earth and all things that are in them.

Most High designates a state of supreme exaltation in rank, power, and dignity.

Redeemer signifies that He has ransomed and will redeem all people from the fall of Adam and from their individual sins.

How many people in the Book of Mormon are named as seeing the Savior?

Although many holy men living in the western hemisphere knew of, spoke of, and wrote of Christ—and thousands saw the Lord in the land of Bountiful (see 3 Ne. 11), as did throngs of Jaredites (see Ether 12:19)—only a few who saw Him are named. Twenty-two men are referred to by name in the Book of Mormon as having seen the Son of God: the brother of Jared (see Ether 3:15), King Emer (see Ether 9:22), Ether (see Ether 13:4), Lehi (see 1 Ne. 1:8–9), Nephi (see 1 Ne. 11:1), Jacob (see 2 Ne. 2:4), King Lamoni (see Alma 19:13), Alma (see Alma 36:22), Mormon (see Morm.

The brother of Jared sees the finger of the Lord

1:15), Moroni (see Ether 12:39), and His Nephite disciples—Nephi (brother to Timothy), Timothy, Jonas, Mathoni, Mathonihah, Kumen, Kumenonhi, Jeremiah, Shemnon, Jonas, Zedekiah, and Isaiah (see 3 Ne. 19:4). Of the twenty-two men, three were Jaredites—the brother of Jared, King Emer, and Ether. The other nineteen were descendants of Lehi.

What are the instructive parallels between Christ's separate appearances to the three Jaredites and His appearances to Lehi's nineteen descendants?

There are at least four instructive parallels. First, the founders of each civilization saw Christ before arriving in the promised land: the brother of Jared (see Ether 3:6–15) and Lehi (1 Ne. 1:8–9). Second, a king within each culture was privileged to see the Lord Jesus: Emer (see Ether 9:22), Nephi (2 Ne. 5:18), and Lamoni (see Alma 19:13). Third, the last known prophet of each fallen civilization received a manifestation of Christ: Moroni (see Ether 12:39) and Ether (see Ether 13:4). Fourth, throngs in both cultures saw the Lord: the

Christ visiting the Americas

Jaredites (see Ether 12:19) and a multitude at the temple in the land of Bountiful (see 3 Ne. 11:16–17).

Was the account of Jesus ministering in the land of Bountiful recorded before the four Gospels of the New Testament were written?

Jesus ministered for three days among the righteous Nephites after His resurrection. Although His visitation in the Americas followed His resurrection in the Holy Land, the account of His visit in 3 Nephi was probably written before the Gospels were written. At issue is the variance among scholars as to the dating of the Gospels. Traditional dates for the writing of the Four Gospels are: Matthew, AD 75–80; Mark, AD 65–70; Luke, AD 80–85; and John, AD 95–100. (*Note:* 1 Ne. 13:24 suggests that the Gospels were written earlier than purported by traditional dates.)[60]

What is the difference between the ministry of Jesus in the Old World and His ministry in the New World?

Although Jesus appeared to multitudes in both hemispheres, there is a marked contrast in the effect of His ministry in the Old and New Worlds. In the land of Jerusalem, the Beloved Son of God was born (see Matt. 1:23), baptized (see Matt. 3:13), crucified (see Matt. 20:19), and resurrected (see Mark 16:9). Yet multitudes who saw and heard Him did not recognize Him as the Son of God. They were "astonished [during his youth] at his understanding and answers" (Luke 2:47), acknowledged Him as a healer (see Mark 1:40–45), feasted on the food He procured (see John 6:5–14), and marveled at His casting out of devils from the besieged (see Mark 9:25). Yet to them Jesus was not the Son of God (see Luke 4:24). To the Apostle Peter, Jesus asked, "But whom say ye that I am? And Simon Peter answered and said, Thou art the Christ, the Son of the living God" (Matt. 16:15–16).

Like Peter, a multitude in the land of Bountiful in AD 34 clearly saw, heard, and acknowledged divine instruction from a Man they knew to be the epitome of righteousness— Jesus Christ, the Son of God.

In the year AD 34 multitudes saw and heard the resurrected Lord and recognized Him as the Mediator, Redeemer, and Chosen One of Israel. They were "all converted unto the Lord, upon all the face of the land" (4 Ne. 1:2). Their conversion and knowledge of Jesus Christ led to nearly two hundred years of continuous peace and prosperity among the Nephites (see 4 Ne. 1:22–23).

How does information about the life and ministry of Jesus Christ contained in the Book of Mormon differ from information about Christ given in the Gospels?

The Gospels of Matthew, Mark, Luke, and John are accounts of the ministry of Jesus Christ, emphasizing His teachings, parables, miracles, Atonement, death, and Resurrection. In contrast, the Book of Mormon explains why the life and teachings of Jesus are so vitally important to the world. In other words, the Gospel writers tell what Jesus did in the Old World. The Book of Mormon writers tell why it was so important that He came to earth

and performed the Atonement to redeem us all.

What can be learned of the ministry of Jesus Christ from reading the Book of Mormon?

Prophetic scribes of the Book of Mormon seemed to delight in writing of the Savior's ministry in the Old World. They wrote of His coming to earth (see 1 Ne. 12:6), His Eternal Father (see 1 Ne. 11:21), and His mortal mother (see Mosiah 3:8). They wrote of His birth (see 1 Ne. 10:4), baptism (see 2 Ne. 31:4), ministry (see 2 Ne. 2:4), disciples (see 1 Ne. 1:10), Atonement (see Jacob 4:11), suffering and death (see 1 Ne. 10:11), and Resurrection (see 2 Ne. 2:8).

The central theme of the Book of Mormon writers was the Atonement of Jesus Christ. Without His atoning sacrifice, the entire plan of salvation would have been thwarted, and the purposes of the Creation, including the populating of the earth, would have been for naught. The Prophet Joseph Smith taught, "All other things which pertain to our religion

Christ teaching the Nephites

are only appendages to [the Atonement]."[61] Elder Bruce R. McConkie said, "Nothing in the entire plan of salvation compares in any way in importance with that most transcendent of all events."[62] Because of the Atonement of Jesus, we are ransomed from the effects of the Fall of Adam. Spiritual and temporal death are overcome through Christ, our victorious Deliverer.

What is the meaning of the "fulness of the gospel of Jesus Christ"?

The word *gospel* in Greek means "good news." The word *gospel* also means "God's story" and "good tidings." Using these definitions, the Book of Mormon contains the fulness of the gospel. Scholar Daniel H. Ludlow added another definition. He wrote, "The fulness of the gospel means that it contains those instructions a person needs to observe in order to be worthy to enter the presence of God in the celestial kingdom."[63]

Does the Book of Mormon focus on blessings for following the teachings of Jesus Christ or on punishments for failing to follow His teachings?

Less than one-fourth of the prophetic writings in the Book of Mormon tell of the positive effects that occur when ancient Americans followed the teachings of Christ. Most of the Book of Mormon record is dominated by war, famine, and destruction because most of the time the Nephites, Lamanites, and Jaredites rejected the Savior and His teachings.

Why did ancient Americans reject the teachings of Jesus?

The ancient Americans did not reject Jesus in ignorance. The Lord did not leave His people in darkness about His will and teachings; rather, the burden of responsibility was on the ancient inhabitants of the Americas. They were taught the gospel but chose to reject a Christ-centered life. The recurring theme of flat rejection of Christ by Nephites, Lamanites, and Jaredites may lead readers to conclude that the Book of Mormon is little more than a methodical course for spiritual failure. That conclusion, however, would be incorrect. The Book of Mormon not only clearly defines a path for spiritual and material ruin, it presents the narrow path

that leads to spiritual well-being. A few faithful followers found the narrow path and emulated the life of Christ. They sought to declare the word of God (see Mosiah 3:3). Through the words of God they brought peace to a war-torn land (see W of M 1:18). They exhorted their people to be faithful and to repent of their sins (see Hel. 6:4). And they testified boldly about the redemption of the Lord (see 3 Ne. 6:20).

What is the purpose and/or most valuable element to be found in the Book of Mormon?

The most valuable element in the Book of Mormon is the ministry and teachings of Jesus. There are 751 verses in the Book of Mormon that "contain distinct instances of divine speech texts." This means "12.6 percent of the Book of Mormon, or, taken as a whole, one verse in every eight" contains speech texts from and about Jesus Christ.[64] By finding the central message of the Book of Mormon, readers comprehend the reason that has moved missionaries, pioneers, and other Latter-day Saints to share the Book of Mormon with the world.

If readers seek to know, they will find that the Book of Mormon prophetic scribes wrote primarily about our Savior. They wrote of Christ because they knew of Him and loved Him. They did not gain their knowledge through a comparison of the customs, characteristics, lifestyles, and mannerisms of Lehi's family with those living in the land of Jerusalem in 600 BC, nor did they gain knowledge of Jesus through findings unearthed by archaeologists, such as skeletal remains, gold plates, cement highways, and places of worship in the Americas. They did not grasp their knowledge of Jesus through acquaintance with Indian traditions, folklore, or legends of voyages and wars. The prophetic scribes gained their knowledge by faith in the life, commandments, and teachings of Jesus Christ.

Why should readers of the Book of Mormon seek to learn more about the Savior?

Perhaps a few polite scholars or the curious might read the Book of Mormon for superficial reasons, but only a promise of deeply significant effects would induce

people around the world to read the pages of the Book of Mormon with real intent. In our fast-paced, twenty-first-century lives, most readers would not be inclined to read a double-columned book of more than five hundred pages if it were presented merely as something of interest to the scholar, curious, or well-meaning.

But if readers recognize that through pondering the central message of the Book of Mormon they could comprehend Jesus the Christ as they could in no other way, they would unlock for themselves a path to greater understanding of the words of God. In that process, they would learn how to be Christlike—and would understand why so many read the Book of Mormon on a daily basis. They would know why the Book of Mormon is a guide for the righteous and why the Savior delights in blessing us all.

How many copies of the Book of Mormon are in circulation today?

On August 28, 2008, the Church of Jesus Christ of Latter-day Saints announced that since its first publication in 1830, more than 140 million copies of the Book of Mormon have been published and distributed in 107 languages.[65]

The Book of Mormon has been printed in 107 languages

3

The Small Plates of Nephi

"The Lord God said unto [Nephi]: Make other plates; and thou shalt engraven many things upon them which are good in my sight, for the profit of thy people."

(2 Ne. 5:30)

TITLE PAGE

Who wrote the title page of the Book of Mormon?

Joseph Smith declared, "The title-page of the Book of Mormon is a literal translation, taken from the very last leaf, on the left hand side of the collection or book of plates."[66] Since the record was "sealed by the hand of Moroni," it is presumed that Moroni, son of Mormon, wrote the title page. This supposition is based on the phrase "sealed by the hand of Moroni," and the last paragraph of the title page that begins "an abridgment taken from the Book of Ether, which book was edited by Moroni."[67]

THE FIRST BOOK OF NEPHI

1 Nephi—What is known about the headnote summary at the beginning of 1 Nephi?

All headnotes in the Book of Mormon were inscribed on the plates. Inserts preceding Mosiah 9 and Alma 21 were also inscribed on the plates. Brief summaries at the beginning of each chapter in the Book of Mormon were not engraved on the small plates. The current summary additions were written for the 1981 edition and serve as helps to guide readers of the Book of Mormon.

The chronological dating was added in the 1920 edition of the Book of Mormon by recommendation of an LDS Church committee spearheaded by Elder James E. Talmage. Previous to 1920, chronological dating did not appear in editions of the Book of Mormon.[68]

James E. Talmage

1 Nephi—1 Nephi is written in first-person narrative. How often is that style used in the Book of Mormon?

The small plates of Nephi were written in first-person narrative, as were the books written by Mormon and his son Moroni. First-person narrative fills approximately one-third of the Book of Mormon text. These books begin with "I, Nephi . . .," and "Now behold, I, Jarom. . . ." (In the Old Testament, on the other hand, the book of Nehemiah is the only extensive first-person narrative.) The abridgement of the large plates of Nephi—Mosiah, Alma, Helaman, 3 Nephi, 4 Nephi, and Mormon— is written in third-person narrative and is a commentary about the events.[69]

1 Nephi 1:1—Is the phrase "born of goodly parents" a moral reference or a reference to the socioeconomic status of Father Lehi?

According to Book of Mormon scholar Hugh Nibley, the reference "born of goodly parents" has social overtones connoting wealth. In 600 BC private fortunes were had in Jerusalem:

"the artists no longer work only for the court and the temples . . . they had now to fill orders for a wealthy bourgeoisie."[70] Yet the society in Jerusalem as a whole was agrarian. Raising grains, beans, and vegetables was the norm, not the exception. It appears that Father Lehi (name probably derived from the Hebrew word *Lhy*) was in a better economic position than the majority in the Holy City due to his holdings in Jerusalem and his land of inheritance beyond the borders of Jerusalem.[71]

1 Nephi 1:1—What did Nephi learn from Father Lehi?

Although Nephi writes, "I was taught somewhat in all the learning of my father," he does not specify what he learned. A review of his writings in 1 Nephi and 2 Nephi reveals that Nephi knew something of carpentry, metallurgy, hunting, and architecture. He was also acquainted with Jewish law and schooled in the Egyptian language. More importantly, however, Nephi knew of the goodness of God.[72] The name *Nephi* may derive from the Egyptian *nfr*, meaning "good," "goodly," and "fair" (1 Ne. 1:1).[73]

1 Nephi 1:2— As Nephi wrote his record on the small plates, he combined the "learning of the Jews and the language of the Egyptians." According to Mormon 9:32–33, inscriptions on the plates were written in reformed Egyptian. What was the writing style used to create reformed Egyptian?

Scholars purport that reformed Egyptian was a type of shorthand. Their reasoning is based on Moroni's explanation that "if our plates had been sufficiently large we should have written in Hebrew" (Morm. 9:33). Hebrew is an alphabetical language, whereas the Egyptian language is not alphabetical. Ancient Egyptians used three writing systems. According to Book of Mormon scholars Stephen Ricks and John A. Tvedtnes, "The hieroglyphs (Greek for 'sacred symbols'), comprised nearly 400 picture characters depicting things found in real life. A cursive script called hieratic (Greek for 'sacred') was also used, principally on papyrus. Around 700 B.C., the Egyptians developed an even more cursive script that we call demotic (Greek for 'popular'), which bore little resemblance to the hieroglyphs."74 As for which writing system was used in engraving the plates, Joseph Smith said that he "translated the book of Mormon from hieroglyphics, the knowledge of which was lost to the world."75 Scholars debate the definition of *hieroglyphs*.

1 Nephi 1:4—When was Zedekiah appointed king of Judah?

According to the Old Testament, Zedekiah—known as Mattaniah, the son of Josiah and Hamutal—was twenty-one years old when he was appointed king over the small vassal state of Judah by Nebuchadnezzar of Babylon (see 2 Chron. 36:11–21; 2 Kgs. 24:17–20). The exact date of his appointment is not known. However, it is known that Lehi and his family fled from Jerusalem in "the first year of the reign of Zedekiah, king of Judah," which suggests that Zedekiah's appointment as king of Judah was about 600 BC (see 1 Ne. 1:4; 1 Ne. 2:1–4).76

1 Nephi 1:4—What were the political issues that led prophets like Jeremiah to prophesy destruction of the Holy City during the reign of King Zedekiah?

Zedekiah's reign proved very disruptive to himself and to Judah. Rather than show allegiance to Babylon, Zedekiah courted an alliance with Egypt in hopes of breaking ties with Babylon. Jeremiah, Nahum, Habakkuk, and Zephaniah were among many prophets who warned against such an alliance (see Jer. 35:15). Jeremiah was particularly vocal.

Statue of the prophet Jeremiah at the Salisbury Cathedral

He prophesied that attempts to form a union with Egypt would lead to the destruction of Jerusalem and the holy temple. He foretold of Babylonian captivity for the people of Judah unless they repented and turned from their evil ways. Jeremiah's message of doom was considered traitorous against Judah; he was captured and placed in prison for his prophesies and strong stance against an Egyptian alliance (see Jer. 26–29). His message, and that of other prophets, was an outrage to Zedekiah and the economic and political leaders of Judah, who saw an alliance with Egypt as the only way to rid Judah of Babylonian rule (see 2 Kgs. 23–25; 2 Chron. 36).[77]

Nebuchadnezzar reacted to the rebellion by sending an army to camp outside the walls of Jerusalem. Then the battles began. After a long siege in which many died, the Holy City fell to Babylon. As for King Zedekiah, he attempted to escape from Babylonian soldiers but was overtaken. He was forced to watch the killing of his sons before the soldiers blinded him. (His son Mulek escaped execution and brought a group from Jerusalem to the Americas [see Omni 1:14–15].) Zedekiah was later bound with brass chains and taken like a "trophy of war" to Babylon (see 2 Kgs. 25:7). Also taken to Babylon were the treasures of the holy temple.[78]

1 Nephi 1:4—Why did King Zedekiah rebel against Babylonian rule in spite of prophetic warnings to the contrary?

Soon after Father Lehi took his family into the wilderness, Zedekiah rebelled against Babylon (see 1 Ne. 2:2; 2 Kgs. 24:18–20). Zedekiah's rebellion took place on the promise of Egyptian support but before that support arrived at Jerusalem.

1 Nephi 1:6—Why is the "pillar of fire" that Lehi saw significant to his call as a prophet of God?

In the scriptures, fire is an agent of purification. For example, when baptized by fire and the Holy Ghost, fire burns sin out of the individual.[79] A pillar of fire or a shaft of light is spoken of in scriptures as an agent of purification when receiving visions, guidance, and protection (see Ex. 13:21–22; Ex. 14:24; Hel. 5:24, 43). In the prophetic call of Father Lehi, the pillar of fire "dwelt upon a rock before him"—a symbol of the Lord's presence (1 Ne. 1:6). It was after seeing the pillar of fire that Lehi "saw and heard much; and because of the things which he saw and heard he did quake and tremble exceedingly" (1 Ne. 1:6).

1 Nephi 1:8—How many of Father Lehi's dreams were recorded by his son Nephi on the small plates?

Seven of Lehi's dreams or visions were recorded by Nephi; these dreams show evidence that Father Lehi was a "visionary man" (1 Ne. 5:4). The recorded dreams may be only representative of other heavenly manifestations, for Nephi wrote, "[Lehi] hath written many things which he saw in visions and in dreams" (1 Ne. 1:16), an indication that the book of Lehi contained other dreams and visions. Father Lehi was not only a "visionary man," but his prophetic words are "some of the most powerful doctrine

and far-reaching prophecies in the entire Book of Mormon. Much of what we know about such basic gospel doctrines as the Fall, the expected Savior, and the house of Israel, we learn from Lehi."[80]

1 Nephi 1:11— In vision Lehi was given a book to read. Was the book bound or was it a scroll?

It is assumed that "the book of prophecy given to Lehi was likely a scroll since there were not bound books at the time" (see Jer. 36:2).[81] It was proper in ancient context to refer to scrolls as books.

1 Nephi 1:16—Is there a name for the historical period in which Lehi lived?

Hugh Nibley wrote of Lehi living in the "Axial Age," a "period extending roughly from the seventh through the fourth centuries B.C., in which a series of prophets and sages, including Zoroaster, Confucius, Buddha, the authors of the Upanishads, the Greek philosophers, and the great Israelite prophets, established fundamentally new

Scroll assumed to be like that given to Lehi to read

paradigms of social and religious thought which formed the ideological basis for nearly all of the subsequent major civilizations of the world."[82]

1 Nephi 1:17—When did Nephi abridge the records of Lehi?

Nephi did not write on the small plates until 570 BC, thirty years after he and his family left the land of Jerusalem (see 2 Ne. 5:28–31). (The large plates of Nephi were created twenty years earlier in 590 BC [see 1 Ne. 19:1–4].) In recreating the wilderness events and the settling of his family in the promised land, it is presumed that Nephi "most likely referred to what had been put down on the larger, 'historical' plates or on perishable materials." If this was the case, "he could pick and choose information from those earlier sources and shape it any way he saw fit."[83] What appears unusual in the historical narrative is that Nephi omitted any mention of other people that he or his family interacted with in the wilderness and the promised land. Certainly in the wilderness, the family passed by other sojourners.[84]

> 1 Nephi 1:17—At this point in the narrative, the large and small plates of Nephi as well as the plates of Laban have been introduced. How many other plates are mentioned in the Book of Mormon?

The *plates of brass* were obtained by Nephi from Laban's servant Zoram in Jerusalem. These plates were regarded as scripture by the Nephites. The plates were written in the Egyptian language (see Mosiah 1:3–4) and kept for generations by the descendants of Joseph of Egypt (see 1 Ne. 5:14–17). Although Joseph Smith never

translated the plates of brass, some of the writings on these plates are found in the Book of Mormon. For example, Nephi and Jacob engraved the words of the ancient prophets Zenos and Isaiah, whose words were written on the plates of brass long before they were engraved on the small plates (see 1 Ne. 3:20; Hel. 8:19–20).

The *large plates of Nephi* were begun soon after Lehi and his family arrived in the promised land. These plates contain a record of the Nephites from about 590 BC to AD 385 (see 1 Ne. 19:1–4). The purpose for writing on the large plates was to keep a secular or temporal history of Lehi and his family as well as their descendants for generations. Although the focus of the large plates was historical in nature, the plates also contain some religious matter (see 1 Ne. 19:4; Jacob 3:13). The books on the large plates include Lehi, Mosiah, Alma, Helaman, 3 Nephi, 4 Nephi, and Mormon. Mormon abridged the account written on the large plates of Nephi, and wrote his abridgment on the *plates of Mormon*. Joseph Smith never translated the large plates of Nephi, but did translate

Mormon's abridgement of the large plates.

The *small plates of Nephi* contain the religious record of the Nephites from about 570 BC to 130 BC (see 2 Ne. 5:39–41). The books on the small plates are 1 Nephi, 2 Nephi, Jacob, Enos, Jarom, and Omni. Joseph Smith was commanded to translate the small plates after the loss of the 116-page manuscript of the book of Lehi.

The *plates of Ether* contain a temporal and religious history of Jared and his people from the great Tower of Babel to the days of the prophetic scribe Ether. These plates were not translated by Joseph Smith. Joseph translated the abridged record of the plates of Ether created by Moroni (see Ether 1:1–2). A portion of the plates of Ether was sealed by the hand of Moroni in obedience to the directions of God. Joseph Smith was told not to translate the sealed portion of this record (see Ether 4:1–4).

The *plates of Mormon* were begun by Mormon and finished by Moroni. These plates contain an abridgment of the large plates of Nephi, the writings of Mormon and his son Moroni,

Moroni's translation of the book of Ether, and the title page of the Book of Mormon (see 3 Ne. 5:8–11). Joseph Smith was given the plates of Mormon by the angel Moroni on September 22, 1827, at the Hill Cumorah.[85]

1 Nephi 1:20—In the very same verse where Nephi tells of Jews seeking to take the life of his father, he writes of the "tender mercies of the Lord." Why?

A repetitive theme expressed by Nephi and other prophetic recorders of the Book of Mormon is that "the tender mercies of the Lord are over all those whom he hath chosen, because of their faith, to make them mighty even unto the power of deliverance" (1 Ne. 1:20). Nephi writes brief vignettes about the tender mercies of God during the wilderness journey and on the high seas, just as other Book of Mormon prophets write of God's mercies during times of war and discord. Their prophetic writings illustrate that obstacles, even deliverance from bondage, can be overcome by the tender mercies of God.[86]

1 Nephi 2:2–4—As Lehi and his family fled into the wilderness, they left their home in Jerusalem and their land of inheritance. What was the Holy City like at the time of their escape into the wilderness? Is there any information about where Lehi's land of inheritance was located?

When Lehi and his family fled into the wilderness, Jerusalem had about 25,000 residents. The famed walls of the city stood about fifteen feet high. As for Lehi's land of inheritance, scholars John Welch and David Seely suggest that it was located about thirty miles north of Jerusalem in western Manasseh, "since it was the only area west of Jordon where Judah had reasserted control." They further suggest that "Lehi owned by virtue of having inherited a deed to the property and which he probably visited on occasion in order to manage the affairs of the land."[87] Scholar Jeffrey R. Chadwick purports that Lehi lived in the Mishneh quarter of Jerusalem.[88]

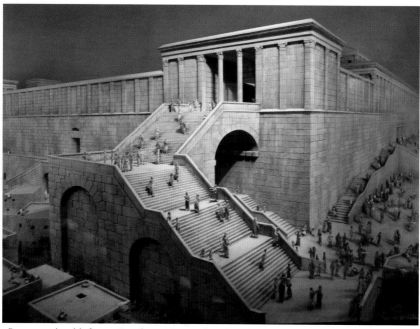

Reconstructed model of ancient Jerusalem in Museum of David Castle

1 Nephi 2:2–4—How might the flight of Lehi and his family into the wilderness serve as both a literal and figurative paradox?

In writing of Lehi and his family leaving Jerusalem and entering the desertlike wilderness, Hugh Nibley said, "The flight from the wicked world and wandering in the wilderness is by no means a unique event, but takes place in every dispensation. . . . Though the righteous go into the desert, it is the wicked who are cut off and lost; it is they who are put under quarantine. . . . It is the Jews at Jerusalem who are left behind and abandoned."[89] Nibley adds, "The desert has two faces; it is a place both of death and of refuge, of defeat and victory, a grim coming-down from Eden and yet a sure escape from the wicked world, the asylum alike of the righteous and the rascal. The pilgrims' way leads through sand and desolation, but it is the way back to paradise; in the desert we lose ourselves to find ourselves. These familiar paradoxes are literal as well as figurative."[90]

1 Nephi 2:4—Was Lehi a collector or an artisan of metals?

Lehi owned gold, silver, and "precious things" (1 Ne. 2:4), the value or worth of which was determined by weight. Lehi's ownership of a variety of metals was a sign of his wealth (see 1 Ne. 3:24). When his family left their "precious things" in the land of their inheritance, it is assumed that they buried their treasures for "a common practice during the Iron Age II period, when Lehi lived, was to place loose silver in ceramic jugs and then bury those containers for safekeeping."[91] Hugh Nibley suggests that the relationship of Lehi and his sons "to fine workmanship and precious materials had been that of handlers and owners but not of artisans and craftsmen."[92] Although Nibley further suggests that it was not until Lehi's family left Jerusalem that the skill of working with metal was acquired, other scholars disagree (see 1 Ne. 17:9–10; 1 Ne. 19:1; 2 Ne. 5:14–15).[93]

1 Nephi 2:5—In what direction did Lehi and his family travel as they fled into the wilderness?

The exact route taken by Lehi and his family is unknown. Scholar S. Kent Brown suggests that there were four possible routes that Lehi could have taken. One route has the family departing through the Jordan Valley and climbing the hills of Moab to reach the King's Highway before turning south. A second route has the family going east beyond the King's Highway to reach a road that would take them south toward the Red Sea. The third possible route has the family traveling to the Ein Gedi oasis before entering a southern trail, and the last route has the family traveling south of the Ein Gedi oasis.[94] Regardless of the route taken (perhaps none of those mentioned), travel from Jerusalem to the Red Sea (the Gulf of Aquaba) is about 180 miles through dry and desolate country. Lehi and his family journeyed three days beyond that point (see 1 Ne. 2:5–6). Then they set up a "base camp" near what Brown describes as the northeastern arm of the Red Sea. There they camped in a Bedouin manner using tents as their abodes. Yet twice the sons of Lehi were asked to return to the city of Jerusalem—first to obtain the plates of brass, and second to persuade Ishmael and his family to join Lehi in the wilderness.

In the writings of Franklin D. Richards and James A. Little is a presumed revelation of Joseph Smith on the travels of Lehi and his family in the wilderness. If the revelation is authentic, it sheds an additional insight about the latitude or direction of Lehi's travels: "Lehi's Travels.—Revelation to Joseph the Seer. The course that Lehi and his company traveled from Jerusalem to the place of their destination: They traveled nearly a south, southeast direction until they came to the nineteenth degree of north latitude; then, nearly east to the Sea of Arabia, then sailed in a southeast direction, and landed on the continent of South America, in Chili [Chile], thirty degrees south latitude."[95]

> **1 Nephi 2:6—Why is it written "pitched his tent in a valley by the side of a river of water" instead of "pitched his tent in a valley by the side of a river"?**

In the Middle East, small rivers do not flow year round. During the winter months rain fills thousands of *wadis* or dry streambeds, creating rivers. In

Forest in the Israeli wilderness

the drier months, streambeds are not rivers of water.[96] According to John A. Tvedtnes, "There were rivers flowing in the western part of Arabia, both in Yemen to the south and in the land of Midian to the north, where Lehi encamped beside the river Laman."[97]

1 Nephi 2:7—How does Lehi's building of the "altar of stones" fit with ancient Hebrew customs?

Lehi—like Adam, Abraham, Isaac, and Jacob—built an "altar of stones" (1 Ne. 2:7). Such practice accords with the commandment written in Exodus 20:24–26 and Deuteronomy 27:5–6. "An altar of stones could consist of a pile of uncut, separate, individual stones, whereas a stone altar could denote the use of cut rock, mortar, etc."[98] A stone altar would never do for an obedient Israelite, because a stone altar had pagan overtones. Thus, the Lord told His servant Moses, "And if thou wilt make me an altar of stone, thou shalt not build it of hewn stone: for if thou lift up thy tool upon it, thou hast polluted it" (Ex. 20:25).

1 Nephi 2:7—What was the primary purpose of an altar of stones? Did Lehi's altar conform?

Altars of stone had a twofold purpose. One purpose was to offer sacrifices to God. Another purpose was to provide a place of asylum. In ancient Israel, those accused of committing a serious crime or offense could "flee to an altar of stones to avoid the consequence of their evil deeds, such as being immediately put to death" (Ex. 21:12–14).[99]

1 Nephi 2:8–10—Was it customary for ancient travelers to name rivers and valleys?

In the United States a river and the adjacent river valley often have the same name (for example, the Missouri River and Missouri Valley.) In the days of Lehi, such was not the practice in the Middle East. Ancient Arabs viewed valleys as symbols of permanence. Thus, Lehi said to his son Lemuel, "O that thou mightest be like unto this valley, firm and steadfast" (Ne. 2:10). Hugh Nibley wrote, "The qualities of firmness and steadfastness, of reliable protection, refreshment, and sure refuge when all else fails, which other nations attribute naturally to mountains, the Arabs

Looking across the River Jordan at Jacob's Ford

attribute to valleys." In contrast to the valleys, rivers in the Middle East are not steadfast. Rivers vary from dry to wet, depending on the season. Bedouin travelers held that "any water you may discover, either in your own territory or in the territory of another tribe is named after you." Thus rivers at different points along their routes were known by different names. "By what right do these people rename streams and valleys to suit themselves?" Hugh Nibley asked before answering, "By the immemorial custom of the desert, to be sure."[100]

> 1 Nephi 2:12—What is the connection in the scriptures between murmuring and divine commands to leave one locale and move to another?

The word *murmur* is found in 1 Nephi during the exodus of Lehi and his family from the land of Jerusalem to the promised land. To "murmur" appears thirty-three times in the Book of Mormon, "nineteen [of which] describe events in the Old World wilderness." In the King James Version of the Old Testament, the world *murmur* appears eighteen times, "all but one of them is connected with the Exodus" of the children of Israel from Egypt and their wanderings in the wilderness for forty years.[101]

> 1 Nephi 2:20—What blessings are associated with the divine promise to "keep the commandments and prosper in the land"?

To *prosper in the land* refers to accumulating great wealth and material possessions. Yet, it may also have reference to the Spirit of the Lord (see D&C 130:20–21; D&C 132:5). Those who rebel against God are "cut off from His presence" and therefore do not prosper in the Spirit of the Lord upon the land (see Alma 38:1).

> 1 Nephi 2:20—Is the reference to "a land which is choice above all other lands" a reference to the United States of America or another country in the Americas?

Some modern-day prophets point to the United States as the "choice land" spoken of in 1 Nephi. President Spencer W. Kimball said, "This America is no ordinary country. It is a choice land, 'choice above all other lands.' (1 Ne. 2:20.) It has a tragic and bloody past, but a glorious and peaceful future if its inhabitants really learn to serve their God."[102] Joseph Fielding Smith added, "They must serve him; they will have to keep his commandments; at least they will have to have some semblance of righteousness or when the fullness of wickedness comes, he certainly will remove them."[103] President Ezra Taft Benson said, "Our Father in Heaven planned the coming forth of the Founding Fathers and their form of government as the necessary great prologue leading to the restoration of the gospel. Recall what our Savior Jesus Christ said nearly two thousand years ago when He visited this promised land: [quotes 3 Ne. 21:4]. America, the land of liberty, was to be the Lord's latter-day base of operations for His restored church."[104]

1 Nephi 3:11—What is "casting of lots"?

Casting of lots was an ancient Hebrew practice. According to the Old Testament, casting of lots was a common practice in the Judean culture for generations (see Lev. 16:8; 1 Sam. 14:42; 1 Chron. 26:13). The practice continued in the New Testament era. For example, lots were cast to determine which member of a particular priestly course had the privilege of entering the temple sanctuary and burning incense. According to the Gospel of Luke, the elderly priest Zacharias was selected by the casting of lots to enter the holy temple. Although elderly, he was not disqualified by age or infirmity from the honor (see Luke 1:9). As to casting of lots in the Nephite narrative, it seems fitting that the firstborn son, Laman, drew the lot, giving him opportunity to fulfill his position in the family.

1 Nephi 3:24—Why is there no reference to "brass plates" in the Book of Mormon? The reference is always stated, "plates of brass."

According to scholar Daniel Ludlow, "In many of the Semitic languages (from which we get the thought patterns contained in the Book of Mormon) it is not

The Copper Scroll found with the Dead Sea Scrolls—an example of ancient records recorded on metal

customary to have the adjective precede the noun. Thus the Book of Mormon mentions the 'plates of brass' of Laban but never refers to the 'brass plates of Laban.'"[105] (Other Semitic phrases like *altar of stone*s are found throughout the Book of Mormon.)

Obtaining the plates of brass proved very important to the Nephite civilization. The plates were written in Egyptian—or, as the scriptures say, Lehi had "been taught in the language of the Egyptians therefore he could read" (Mosiah 1:4). The plates set a pattern for the use of Egyptian script (reformed Egyptian) for scribes of the small and large plates and the writings of Mormon and Moroni (see Mosiah 1:4; Morm. 9:32). The plates also served as a standard

for protecting and preserving the Nephite language (see 1 Ne. 3:19; Morm. 9:33). Of the plates of brass, Elder Bruce R. McConkie wrote, "From prophet to prophet and generation to generation the Brass Plates were handed down and preserved by the Nephites (Mosiah 1:16; 3 Ne. 1:2). At some future date the Lord has promised to bring them forth, undimmed by time and retaining their original brightness, and the scriptural accounts recorded on them are to 'go forth unto every nation, kindred, tongue, and people'" (see Alma 37:3–5; 1 Ne. 5:18–19).[106]

1 Ne. 3:24—What writings are contained on the plates of brass?

The first five books of the Old Testament—Genesis, Exodus, Leviticus, Numbers, and Deuteronomy—are engraved on the plates of brass. In addition, the plates of brass included a history "of the Jews . . . down to the commencement of the reign of Zedekiah" and "the prophecies of the holy prophets," which must certainly have included the words of Zenock, Neum, and Zenos (1 Ne. 5:12–13). Of these prophets, Zenos was the most quoted by the ancient recorders (see 1 Ne. 19:10–17; Jacob 5:1; 3 Ne. 10:16). In fact, next to the prophet Isaiah, Zenos was "the most conspicuous Old World prophetic figure" in the Book of Mormon.[107] A genealogy of the progenitors of Lehi down to Joseph, who was sold into Egypt, is also engraved on the plates of brass (see 1 Ne. 5:10–16).

1 Nephi 3:31—What military status does commanding a garrison of fifty soldiers give Laban?

A garrison of fifty men seems small for the city of Jerusalem, which boasted 25,000 residents at the time. Nephi assures his brothers that God is "mightier than Laban and his fifty" before adding "or even than his tens of thousands" (1 Ne. 4:1). The last statement suggests that Laban had "his tens of thousands in the field, but such an array is of no concern to Laman and Lemuel: it is the 'fifty' they must look out for—the regular, permanent garrison of Jerusalem."[108] Hugh Nibley points out that Laban "commanded a garrison of fifty, that he met in full ceremonial armor with 'the elders of the Jews' for secret consultations by night, that he had control of a treasury, that he was of the old aristocracy, being a distant relative to Lehi himself, that he probably held his job because of his ancestors . . . that his house was the storing place of very old records, that he was a large man, short-tempered, crafty, and dangerous, add to the bargain cruel, greedy, unscrupulous, weak, and given to drink."[109]

1 Nephi 4:9—Why did the sword of Laban gain such prominence among later generations of Nephites?

The sword of Laban was kept with the precious treasures of the Nephites such as the Liahona,

64

plates of brass, and plates of Nephi. The sword was passed to Nephite leaders from generation to generation. This indicates that the sword of Laban had apparent value to the Nephites. Only rulers of the Nephites wielded the sword of Laban (see Jacob 1:10; W of M 1:13; Alma 2:29, 31). The sword was used as a pattern for making other swords (see 1 Ne. 4:9, 18–19; 2 Ne. 5:14).

In addition, the sword of Laban was used to symbolize the word of God.[110] The fact that the sword has two edges shows that "the word of the Lord can bring either salvation or destruction, depending on whether we wield it or are judged by it" (Rev. 1:16; see also Rev. 2:12, 16).[111] Wielding the sword shows a willingness to fight sin and corruption.

1 Nephi 4:20—What was Zoram's role in Laban's household?

Zoram is considered to be the private secretary of Laban and the keeper of the keys, which made him "an important official and no mere slave." He held an honorable position as a servant or "official representative" of Laban.[112] Zoram should not be viewed as a lowly servant who washed the feet of those who entered Laban's dwelling.

1 Nephi 4:22, 26—Were the "elders of the Jews" leading men of Jerusalem or leaders of the Israelite faith?

The word *elders* or *zeqanium* is not a reference to a priesthood office. "Elders of the Jews" are considered to be "the heads of the most influential families of a city." In each city of Judah, elders composed the "ruling body and represented the voice of the free and traditionally independent citizenry . . . in the capital city they were a check on the king himself, and in Jerusalem no king could be crowned without their approval or pass important laws without their consent."[113] Perhaps Laban was one of the leading elders of Jerusalem as well as a military leader.

1 Nephi 4:32—Why is the phrase "as the Lord liveth, and as I live" so binding on Nephi in his relationship with Zoram?

The phrase is an ancient oath or promise from one man to another (see Num. 14:21; Jer. 46:18).

"There is nothing stronger, and nothing more sacred than the oath among the nomads . . . the taking of an oath is a holy thing with the Bedouins, wo[e] to him who swears falsely; his social standing will be damaged and his reputation ruined. No one will receive his testimony, and he must also pay a money fine." The most binding oath must "be by the life of something, even if it be but a blade of grass. The only oath more awful than that 'by my life' or (less commonly) 'by the life of my head,' is the *wa hayat Allah* 'by the life of God' or 'as the Lord Liveth.'"[114] Thus, when Nephi said to Zoram "as the Lord liveth, and as I live," he assured Zoram that his word was his bond and that Zoram's life would be spared (1 Ne. 4:32–33).

Of this oath Hugh Nibley wrote, "When [Zoram] saw the brethren and heard Nephi's real voice he got the shock of his life and in a panic made a break for the city. In such a situation there was only one thing Nephi could possibly have done, both to spare Zoram and to avoid giving alarm—and no westerner could have guessed what it was. Nephi, a powerful fellow, held the terrified Zoram in a vice-like

grip long enough to swear a solemn oath in his ear, 'as the Lord liveth, and as I live.' . . . As soon as Zoram 'made an oath unto us that he would tarry with us from that time forth . . . our fears did cease concerning him.'"[115]

> 1 Nephi 5:1–3—Before Lehi's sons returned to their base camp, the name of their mother was given. What is the meaning of Sariah?

Book of Mormon scholars George Reynolds and Janne Sjodahl surmise that the name *Sariah* is "a compound of two Hebrew words: 'Sarah-Jah' meaning literally 'Princess of the Lord.'"[116]

> 1 Nephi 5:9—When Lehi's sons returned to the base camp, the family "rejoice[d] exceedingly." In what way were their sacrificial offerings a necessary or customary part of rejoicing?

Since the days of Adam, the children of Israel have offered animal sacrifices to the Lord, symbolic of the atoning sacrifice of Jesus Christ (see Moses 5:5–8). With the safe return of his sons from Jerusalem, Lehi offered a peace offering or thanksgiving offering to God in remembrance of their safe travels like prophetic leaders before him (see Ps. 107:4–8, 19–32). Psalms 107:22 advises that "sacrifices of thanksgiving" must be offered for a safe journey. Lehi offered thanksgiving offerings two other times: first when his family first set up base camp (see 1 Ne. 2:7), and a second time when his sons returned to base camp with Ishmael's family (see 1 Ne. 7:22). Such offerings were specified in the law of Moses.

1 Nephi 5:9—What purpose do burnt offerings serve? Are they related to peace or thanksgiving offerings?

The sacrifice of burnt offerings is different from sacrifices of thanksgiving or peace offerings. The sacrifice of burnt offerings was to mend a relationship between God and His people that had been altered by sin. The burnt offering was to purge sin (see Lev. 4:2–12).[117] Could it be that Lehi wanted to purge the sins of his family when he offered a sacrifice of burnt offerings? Such sins would have included, but were not limited to, difficulties between his sons and the complaints of Sariah.

1 Nephi 5:14—From which tribe in the house of Israel did Lehi descend?

Lehi offers a sacrifice

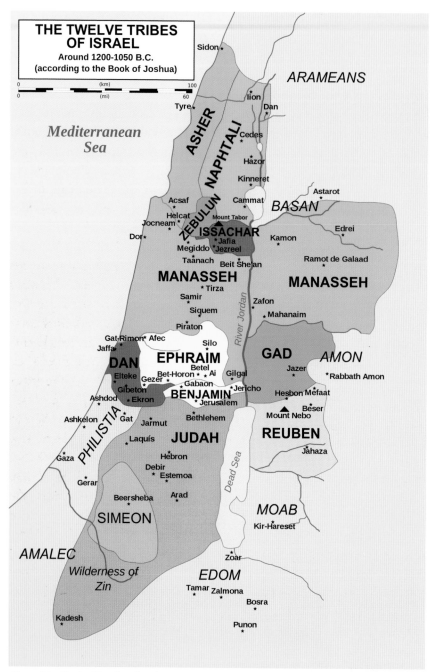

Mediterranean
Sea

ARAMEANS

Sidon

Tyre

Iion

Dan

ASHER

NAPHTALI

Cedes

Hazor

Kinneret

Astarot

Acsaf

Cammat

BASAN

Helcat

ZEBULUN

Mount Tabor

Edrei

Jocneam

ISSACHAR

Dor

Jafia

Kamon

Megiddo

Jezreel

Taanach

Beit She'an

Ramot de Galaad

MANASSEH

MANASSEH

Tirza

Samir

Zafon

Siquem

Mahanaim

River Jordan

Piraton

Gat-Rimon

Afec

Silo

Jaffa

EPHRAIM

GAD

AMON

Betel

Elteke

Bet-Horon

Ai

Gilgal

Jazer

Rabbath Amon

DAN

Gezer

Gibeton

Gabaon

Jericho

Hesbon

Mefaat

Ashdod

Ekron

BENJAMIN

Beser

Ashkelon

Gat

Jerusalem

Mount Nebo

Jarmut

Bethlehem

REUBEN

PHILISTIA

JUDAH

Laquís

Gaza

Hebron

Jahaza

Debir

Estemoa

Gerar

Dead Sea

Beersheba

Arad

MOAB

SIMEON

Kir-Hareset

AMALEC

Zoar

Wilderness of
Zin

EDOM

Tamar

Zalmona

Bosra

Kadesh

Punon

The traditional lands of the tribes of Israel

Lehi was a descendant of Manasseh, the son of Joseph, who was sold into Egypt (see Alma 10:3). Scholars Welch and Seely suggest that "Lehi was probably a descendant of Manassite refugees who had fled south to Judah with others of the northern kingdom when the Assyrians attacked, destroyed, and deported Israel in 724–722 B.C."[118]

1 Nephi 7:2—From which tribe in the house of Israel did Ishmael descend?

On May 6, 1882, in Logan, Utah, Elder Erastus Snow said, "The Prophet Joseph informed us that the record of Lehi was contained on the 116 pages that were first translated and subsequently stolen, and of which an abridgement is given us in the First Book of Nephi, which is the record of Nephi individually, he himself being of the lineage of Manasseh; but that Ishmael was of the lineage of Ephraim, and that his sons married into Lehi's family, and Lehi's sons married Ishmael's daughters, thus fulfilling the words of Jacob upon Ephraim and Manasseh in the 48th chapter of Genesis, which says, 'And let my name be named

on them, and the name of my fathers Abraham and Isaac; and let them grow into a multitude in the midst of the land."[119]

1 Nephi 7:1; 8:1—What role does parallelism play in Lehi's sons taking the daughters of Ishmael "to wife, that they might raise up seed" and Lehi's family gathering "all manner of seeds"?

There is parallelism in the seeds of posterity and the plant seeds of life needed to preserve Lehi's family. It appears that these two related themes occupied Lehi's thoughts before his epic dream (see 1 Ne. 8:1–4). Would the plant seeds survive the tempest to sustain generations of his family? Would his posterity survive doubt (see 1 Ne. 2:12–13), envy (see 1 Ne. 2:22), and hate (see 1 Ne. 2:24)? Would his posterity keep the commandments and covenants of God (see Lev. 19:19; Deut. 22:9–11)? Perhaps as Lehi pondered the outcome of his seed, the Lord saw fit to reveal the eternal plan of salvation in a familial dream.

1 Nephi 8:2—What were the hopes and fears of Lehi's family as they heard his prophetic

Lehi's dreams and the family's reaction to those dreams dominate the first chapters of the Book of Mormon. Previous visionary dreams of Lehi resulted in loss of fortune (see 1 Ne. 2:4) and home (see 1 Ne. 2:2, 4). One dream led the family to camp in the wilderness rather than continue living in the comforts of Jerusalem (see 1 Ne. 2:15). Another dream led Lehi's sons to risk their lives and even take a life to obtain the plates of brass (see 1 Ne. 3, 4). Verbal descriptions of these dreams, while vivid visual experiences to Lehi, were not quickly visualized or appreciated by his sons. Nephi pondered (see 1 Ne. 11:1), and Laman and Lemuel disputed (see 1 Ne. 15:2).

1 Nephi 8:2—What does this familial dream of Lehi teach about the role of a patriarch in the family?

This dream teaches the eternal role of a father and shows how a godly patriarch can guide and devote his life to the salvation of himself and his family through Jesus Christ. It portrays Lehi first seeing and reaching out to his wife, Sariah. Sariah responds and joins him at the tree in the love of God. Lehi then reaches out to his children. Some of his children embrace his entreaties and join him at the tree. When other children reject his entreaties, Lehi searches to understand the world and its follies so that he can warn his children of imminent dangers that await their perilous choice. He persists in faith and love, praying that someday in God's mercy his children will hear him and reach for the rod—the word of God—to lead them to eternal life (see Alma 37:43–44).

1 Nephi 8:5—In Lehi's dream, what is the significance of the man dressed in a white robe?

Lehi saw himself and perhaps all mankind beginning their journey in the "dark and dreary wilderness" (1 Ne. 8:4). Lehi knew that he must find his way back to the light and life of Christ, and escape the loneliness of the dark. A man dressed in contrasting white "came and stood before [Lehi]" (1 Ne. 8:5). The man "bade [Lehi to] follow him" (1 Ne. 8:6). This man—whether a messenger from the throne of God, the Holy Ghost, or Jesus the Christ—led Father Lehi through the dark and dreary waste. The man's words were a symbolic representation of Christ's words, "Follow me" (Matt. 4:19; 2 Ne. 31:10). Though Lehi followed his guide obediently and with childlike faith, he yearned for greater light and prayed for mercy. It was then that his guide showed Lehi the "large and spacious field."

1 Nephi 8:9—What was the nature of the "large and spacious field"? Was it a safe place?

A later and closer look at the field revealed its deceptive, satanic perils. However, at this point in his dream Lehi's "mind [was so] swallowed up in other things" that Lucifer's seductive lights and snares went unnoticed (1 Ne. 15:27).

1 Nephi 8:10—What is the significance of Lehi seeing "a tree, whose fruit was desirable to make one happy"?

In the tree, Lehi sees the culmination of the seed: a fruit-bearing tree. This tree yields fruit to cure every ill, to extend love to all, and to signal the ultimate destination of the eternal pathway to godhood (see 1 Ne. 8:11). To Lehi, continual partaking of its life-giving properties or accessing the Atonement through repentance meant eternal life—a life full of the love of God. By partaking of the fruit, Lehi's soul was open to the sweetness of the illuminating light of glorified truth. In the fruit-bearing tree, Lehi found the purpose for traversing the dark avoiding false beacons, in his taste of the love of God.

Milton R. Hunter and Warren Ferguson wrote of the tree as a symbol of life in ancient America: "Before the crucifixion of Christ, the tree of life symbol was used extensively. After the crucifixion the cross seems to have replaced it to a degree."[120]

1 Nephi 8:13–15—Why did Lehi call to Sariah, Sam, and Nephi with a "loud voice"?

Filled with the love of God, Lehi was desirous that his family should partake of the fruit and embrace God's love. Lehi cast his eyes about in hopes that he might discover his family. So filled with the love of God was Lehi that even though he now saw (apparently for the first time) the perilous waters that endangered all who strayed from the strait way he did not note the waters' filth (see 1 Ne. 15:27). The first person that he saw was the mother of his family, Sariah. She had only the last—but surely the darkest and most dangerous—steps ahead to reach the tree. Sariah, joined by Sam and Nephi, hesitated and "stood as if they knew not whither they should go" (1 Ne. 8:14). Lehi knew the course toward

Lehi's dream

great joy. He could not and would not force them. He beckoned them with a loud voice, calling them to come unto him and partake of the fruit (see 1 Ne. 8:15). Hearkening to his sure voice, Sariah, Sam, and Nephi came to him and partook (see 1 Ne. 8:16).

1 Nephi 8:20—What is the significance of Lehi seeing in his dream a "rod of iron" and a "strait and narrow path"?

From his vantage point at the tree, Lehi saw the word of God symbolically represented by a rod

of iron. (In Psalms 2:9 and Revelation 12:5, a *rod* symbolizes ruling power. In other scriptural references, a *rod* is used for the correction and guidance of wayward Israelites [see Lev. 27:32; Ezek. 20:37].)[121] The Egyptian word *mdw* means "'a staff [or] rod' but also 'to speak' a 'word.'"[122] In Lehi's dream, the rod "extended along the bank of the river" (1 Ne. 8:19). The rod led with secured, enduring strength through the spacious field to the tree. Of the rod of iron, President Harold B. Lee said, "Wouldn't it be a great thing if all who are well schooled in secular learning could hold fast to the 'iron rod,' or the word of God, which could lead them, through faith, to an understanding, rather than to have them stray away into strange paths of man-made theories and be plunged into the murky waters of disbelief and apostasy?"[123]

Lehi also saw a strait and narrow path near the river and the rod of iron (see 1 Ne. 8:20). The word *strait* means "a narrow passage" much like the Straits of Gibraltar and Straits of Magellan. Yet the way to the tree or love of God is also a "straight," not a crooked, path (see Alma 37:44; Isa. 40:4).

1 Nephi 8:23, 26—What do the mists of darkness and spacious building represent in Lehi's dream?

The mists of darkness represents the temptations of Satan (see 1 Ne. 12:17). The satanic devices of sin and vice blur the perspectives of the traveler who journeys on the road of life, dulling his sense of human dignity, eroding his integrity, and obscuring his vision of the rod of iron. The spacious building without foundation and without God's light was symbolic of the pride and vain imaginations of the world (see Eph. 2:2). Misguided and deceived multitudes pointed "fingers towards those who had come at and were partaking of the fruit" (1 Ne. 8:27). Such public merriment over a sacred partaking is an affront to God. Satan will not uphold his own in their folly and worldly wisdom. His building, the world and wisdom thereof, and his host of subjugated followers will surely fall (see 1 Ne. 11:36; 2 Ne. 9:28–29).

1 Nephi 10:3—In what year did Babylon destroy the holy city of Jerusalem?

Jerusalem was destroyed by the Babylonians in 587 BC; in that battle for the supremacy of Jerusalem, thousands of Jews lost their lives, and survivors were taken as slaves to Babylon. It was not until 523 BC that Babylon was destroyed by the Persian Empire. Under the rule of Cyrus of Persia, the Jews were freed from captivity. Many of the Jews returned to Jerusalem, where they rebuilt their temple to God. They lived in Jerusalem under foreign rule—that of the Persians, Greeks, Asmonaeans, and Romans—for more than five hundred years. In about AD 70 Roman soldiers under the leadership of Titus destroyed Jerusalem, tore down the holy temple, and took the Jewish people as captives to Rome. Later the people of Judah were scattered among the nations.[124]

1 Nephi 11—What other people saw Lehi's dream?

Lehi's dream was seen in part by Nephi and Joseph Smith Sr. Nephi saw the tree bearing fruit, rod of iron, spacious building, mists of darkness, and river of water; he does not mention seeing the strait and narrow path. Joseph Smith Sr. saw the darkened world, narrow path, stream of water, valley, tree bearing fruit, and spacious

Walls of Babylon

building. Of the three who experienced similar dreams, only Joseph Smith Sr. saw his entire family join him at the tree to partake of the fruit. His wife, Lucy Mack Smith, recorded, "the more we ate, the more we seemed to desire, until we even got down upon our knees and scooped it up, eating it by double handfuls." [125] It is presumed that Joseph Smith Sr.'s vision of the tree portrayed the future joy his family would have in accepting the sacred truths of the Book of Mormon.

Mary, mother of Jesus

1 Nephi 11:15—Is the reference to "a virgin, most beautiful and fair above all other virgins" a reference to Mary, the mother of Jesus?

The virgin mentioned in 1 Nephi 11:15 is a reference to Mary, the mother of Jesus. The name *Mary,* a common Hebrew name, means "rebellion" or "bitterness." The name *Mary* is equivalent to *Mara,* the name used by Naomi to describe her perceived misfortunes (see Ruth 1:20). Mary learned of her chosen state from the angel Gabriel, who began his greeting with "Hail Mary." According to the Latin Vulgate version of the Bible, *hail* translates as "ave," which forms the phrase *Ave Maria.* The angelic annunciation to the "most beautiful and fair above all other virgins" included the phrase *highly favoured,* which means "imbued" or "endowed with grace from God" (Luke 1:28). The angel also told Mary that the child to be conceived in her womb was to be begotten of the Eternal Father, "not in violation of natural law but in accordance with a higher manifestation." Mary's reply to the annunciation—"Be it unto me according to thy word"—bespeaks her willingness to obey the will of God and become a handmaiden, meaning "servant of the Lord" (Luke 1:38).[126]

1 Nephi 11:27—Why did the Holy Ghost appear "in the form of a dove" at the baptism of Jesus?

The Prophet Joseph Smith said, "The sign of the dove was instituted before the creation of the world, a witness for the Holy Ghost, and the devil cannot come in the sign of a dove. The Holy Ghost is a personage, and is in the form of a personage. It does not confine itself to the *form* of a dove, but in the *sign* of the dove. The Holy Ghost cannot be transformed into a dove; but the sign of a dove was given to John [the Baptist] to signify the truth of the deed, as the dove is an emblem or token of truth and innocence."[127]

1 Nephi 13:4–6—What is the church of the devil that Nephi saw among the Gentiles?

Elder Bruce R. McConkie wrote, "The Church of the devil is the world; it is all the carnality and evil to which fallen man is heir; it is every unholy and wicked practice; it is every false religion, every supposed system of salvation which does not actually save and exalt man in the highest heaven of the celestial world."[128]

1 Nephi 13:10—What is the definition of a "Gentile"?

The word *Gentile*—which comes from the Latin *gentiles*—means "nations."[129] The definition of *Gentile,* however, depends on the historical setting or doctrinal teaching in which the word is used. *Gentile* can be used as a reference to the same clan or race. But for the most part, it is a reference to those who do not believe in the God of Israel or are not numbered among the house of Israel. When the Book of Mormon refers to people dwelling in gentile nations, it refers to those who dwell beyond the land of Jerusalem. (There is not one Book of Mormon reference to Lamanites or other dissidents of Father Lehi's family being Gentiles.) Most references in the Book of Mormon to Gentiles refer to those in the latter days who are not of the house of Israel.

1 Nephi 13:12—Who is Nephi writing about when he tells of "a man among the Gentiles" who goes upon the waters to the promised land?

In reference to 1 Nephi 13:12, President Ezra Taft Benson taught, "That man, of course, was Christopher Columbus, who testified that he was inspired in what he did." President Benson then quoted from the writings of Columbus: "From my first youth onward, I was a seaman and have so continued until this day. . . . Wherever on the earth a ship has been, I have been. I have spoken and treated with learned men, priests, and laymen, Latins and Greeks, Jews and Moors, and with many men of other faiths. The Lord was well disposed to my desire, and He bestowed upon me courage and understanding; knowledge of seafaring He gave me an abundance, of astrology as much as was needed, and of geometry and astronomy likewise. Further, He gave me joy and cunning in drawing maps and thereon cities, mountains, rivers, islands, and harbours, each one in its place. I have seen and truly I have studied all books—cosmographies, histories, chronicles, and philosophies, and other arts, for which our Lord unlocked my mind, sent me upon the sea, and gave me fire for the deed. Those who heard of my enterprise called it foolish, mocked me, and laughed. But who can doubt but that the Holy Ghost inspired me?" [130]

1 Nephi 13:23—How do Book of Mormon prophetic scribes use the word *Jew* in their writings?

Although the word *Jew* refers to descendants from the tribe of Judah, Book of Mormon scribes use the word *Jew* to refer to any Israelite from the land or kingdom of Judah. Thus, references to *Jew* in the Book of Mormon point to all Israelites, not just those of the tribe of Judah. [131]

1 Nephi 16:7—Why is there such sparse accounting of at least five weddings between the sons and daughters of Lehi and Ishmael?

The five known marriages were those of Nephi, Sam, Laman, Lemuel, and Zoram to the daughters of Ishmael. In antiquity, there was no such thing as courting or even dating. Marriages were negotiated by fathers of the brides and grooms. Most marriages were agreed on when the children were young, which leads to the supposition that Lehi and Ishmael had agreed on the marriages of their children prior to their journey in the wilderness. The marriage custom at the time was seven days of "feasting and merrymaking" over the marriages. It is not known why Nephi chose to withhold details about the marriages between the sons and daughters of Lehi and Ishmael.[132]

> 1 Nephi 16:10—At the door of Lehi's tent was found a ball of curious workmanship known as the Liahona. What is the meaning of *Liahona?*

According to George Reynolds and Janne M. Sjodahl, the word *Liahona* is "Hebrew with an Egyptian ending. . . . *L* is a Hebrew preposition meaning 'to,' and sometimes used to express the possessive case. *Iah* is a Hebrew abbreviated form of 'Jehovah,' common in Hebrew names. *On* is the Hebrew name of the Egyptian 'City of the Sun' . . . *L-iah-on* means, therefore, literally, 'To God is Light' or, 'of God is Light.' That is to say, God gives light, as does the Sun. The final *a* reminds us that the Egyptian form of the Hebrew name *On* is *Annu,* and that seems to be the form Lehi used."[133] (Note that this interpretation is not accepted by modern Egyptologists.) The Liahona is referred to

Middle-Eastern nomadic camp

as a "compass," showing the way Lehi and his family should travel (see 1 Ne. 16:9–10). George Reynolds noted, "In the days of Moses, when he led the children of Israel out of Egypt a pillar of cloud by day and of fire by night moved in front of them. This the Hebrews followed. But to Lehi he gave this Liahona, or compass, as the ball was called and it pointed the way they should travel. It had one strange peculiarity, which was that it worked according to their faith and diligence. When they kept God's law it showed them much more clearly the way they should go than when they were careless or rebellious."[134]

> **1 Nephi 16:12—What difficulty was experienced when Lehi's family folded up their tents, gathered their possessions, and traveled deeper into the wilderness?**

According to S. Kent Brown, "There can be no doubt that pack animals carried the family's belongings. Each of the 'tents'—and there were several, typically one for each married couple—would have weighed several hundred pounds, far too much

for one person to cart. Moreover, the 'seed of every kind,' which was destined to be planted in the promised land (1 Ne. 18:24), would have required a person to shoulder seed bags commonly weighing in excess of 150 pounds." Brown concludes that as the family traveled, "Time needed both to set up camp properly in the evening and then to strike camp in the morning would dictate that, as long as the party was on the march, they would not pitch tents and unpack all of their gear for a night. Instead, family members would have wrapped themselves in blankets or rugs and slept on the ground. . . . Only when party members 'did pitch our tents' in order to 'rest ourselves and to obtain food' for several days or longer did they unpack tents and other materials" (see 1 Ne. 16:17).[135]

> **1 Nephi 16:13—As Lehi's family moved deeper into the wilderness, what conditions did they find?**

The environment of the southern Arabian peninsula took its toll on Lehi's family. The harsh desert climate was difficult. Per-

Landscape of the Arabian Peninsula

haps more difficult was the fact that they were moving into an area known for its "unfriendly tribesmen and . . . long-standing tribal conflicts."[136]

1 Nephi 16:13—What is the meaning of *Shazer,* the place where Lehi and his family stopped to pitch their tents?

Hugh Nibley writes, "The name [*Shazer*] is intriguing. The combination *shajer* is quite common in Palestinian place names; it is a collective meaning 'trees,' and many Arabs (especially in Egypt) pronounce it *shazher*."[137]

1 Nephi 16:34—Ishmael died and was buried in Nahom. Is the word *Nahom* of Hebrew or Arabic origin?

Nahom may relate to *naham,* a Hebrew verb meaning "to console oneself." The Hebrew word *nahum* means "comfort."

The Arabic root *NHM* means "voracious" or "insatiable" and "gluttonous."[138] In Hebrew, not Arabic, *Nahom* appears an appropriate name for the burial site of Ishmael. S. Kent Brown adds, "From Nephi's language, it seems clear that 'the place' already carried a local name. Its general locale is now known. It lies south of the Wadi Jawf, a place known variously as *Nihm* or *Nehem,* meaning to cut stone and to quarry. Three votive altars, dated to the seventh or sixth centuries B.C., all attest to the antiquity of this tribal and regional name. In effect, these altars offer the first archaeological correlation to specific events noted in the Book of Mormon" (see 1 Ne. 16).[139]

1 Nephi 17:5—After eight years of sojourning in the wilderness, Lehi and his family settled in the land of Bountiful. Is the location of Bountiful known?

S. Kent Brown suggests that the land of Bountiful was in "the Dhofar region in the south of modern Oman." According to Brown, the Dhofar region is "a botanical anomaly in Arabia, a virtual Garden of Eden during the rainy season." Brown claims, "No other region, north or south, matches even remotely the Bountiful described by Nephi."[140]

> **1 Nephi 17:7—How does Nephi's mountain experience correlate to experiences of other prophets? Does the Dhofar region correlate with Nephi's description of the area?**

Throughout antiquity, mountains were places where God communed with man. In essence, mountains are "nature's temple, a point of intercession between the finite and the infinite."[141] In the Dhofar region, "mountains rise precipitously out of the Arabian Sea, some to heights over 5,000 feet, and then run gradually downward and northward toward the sand desert."[142]

> **1 Nephi 17:8—While Nephi was on a mountain the Lord told him to construct a ship. Was Nephi familiar with ships or shipbuilding?**

Although Nephi's brothers never mocked his skills as a hunter, they called him a fool for thinking he could build a ship (see 1 Ne. 17:17). An ancient Mideastern proverb says, "Show an Arab the sea and a man of Sidon the desert."[143] Nephi was much more at home in the desert than on the sea. Yet if Bountiful were along the Dhofar coastline, Nephi would have seen vessels heading for ancient Qana. He may have been aware of an Egyptian expedition to sail around Africa begun the year his family left Jerusalem.[144] But it appears that Nephi was not trained in the art of shipbuilding. In a positive response to the Lord's command, Nephi—like all prophets before him—showed

Southern Oman

great faith by his willingness to do something extraordinary (see Ex. 4:10–18; Moses 6:31–37). The Lord showed Nephi, like he did Noah, how to construct a ship (see 1 Ne. 17:8).

1 Nephi 17:23–46—Why did Nephi remind Laman and Lemuel of the many mercies of God in delivering the children of Israel from bondage?

For Nephi, remembrance was not passive—instead, it was active. Nephi asked his brothers to recall past events in their minds and hearts to arouse their consciousness so they would trust in God. Nephi wanted his brothers to remember the covenant or binding agreement between Jehovah and Israel. By remembering the mercies of God in dealing with His chosen people, Nephi hoped that his brothers would recommit to love God and keep His commandments. Sadly, Nephi's hope was in vain.

1 Nephi 18:6—What did Lehi and his family take aboard their ship?

Lehi and his family took aboard ship "fruits and meat from the wilderness, and honey in abundance, and provisions" (1 Ne. 18:6). There is no mention of animals being taken aboard ship. It was not until the family reached the promised land that animals were mentioned (see 1 Ne. 18:25).

1 Nephi 18:23—Where in the Americas did Lehi and his family land?

The Church has not taken an official stand on where Lehi and his family landed in the Americas. In 1929, President Anthony W. Ivins said, "There has never been anything yet set forth that definitely settles the question."[145]

Extant historic documents suggest possible landing sites, none of which have been verified. In the papers of Frederick G. Williams, a counselor to the Prophet Joseph Smith, is found the following: "Lehi's Travels—Revelations to Joseph Seer: The course that Lehi and his company traveled from Jerusalem to the place of their destination: They traveled nearly a south, southeast direction until they came to the nineteenth degree of north latitude; then nearly east to the sea of Arabia, then sailed in a southeast direction, and landed on the continent of South America, in Chile, 30 degrees, south latitude."[146]

On the last page of the John M. Bernhisel transcript of the Joseph Smith Translation of the Bible is found, "The course that Lehi traveled from the city of Jerusalem to the place where he and his family took ship. They traveled nearly a south Latitude then nearly East to the sea of Arabia then sailed in a south east direction and landed on the continent of South America in Chili thirty degrees south Lattitude."[147] On September 15, 1842, an editorial in the *Times and Seasons* claimed that "[Lehi] landed a little south of the Isthmus of Darien (Panama)."[148] It should be noted again that there is no official Church stand on where Lehi and his family landed in the Americas.

> **1 Nephi 18:25—Of the variety of beasts found by Lehi and his family in the promised land, why has finding "the horse" proven so controversial?**

When the Book of Mormon was first published in 1830, the scholarly community in the United States claimed that there were no horses in the Americas before the arrival of Columbus. Archaeological discoveries of horselike fossils after the publication of the Book of Mormon suggest the validity of horses among the Nephites.[149]

The Book of Mormon tells of horses being useful to man as early as the days of King Emer, a Jaredite (see Ether 9:19). Of the fourteen different times that the word *horse* is mentioned in the Book of Mormon, there is no reference to a horse being ridden.

> **1 Nephi 19–21—Why did Nephi turn from an historical narrative of his family to quoting ancient prophets? The change seems a dramatic shift from a story line to doctrine.**

Nephi looks to Zenock, Neum, Zenos, and Isaiah to support his doctrinal teachings to

Horse fossil found in North America (Idaho)

Laman and Lemuel. In looking at the writings of Nephi "as a whole and dividing his chapters into categories based upon content, he wrote 21 historic chapters, 18 Isaiah chapters (quoting or paraphrasing Isaiah), 12 teaching chapters, and 5 visionary chapters. Apart from the historical content, the Isaiah chapters comprise the largest selection of material Nephi chose to engrave into the metal plates."[150]

1 Nephi 20–21—What other Isaiah chapters besides 48–49 were quoted in the Book of Mormon?

The other Isaiah chapters quoted by Nephi and his brother Jacob are chapters 2–14, 29, and 50–54. In the Book of Mormon there are twenty-one full chapters of Isaiah besides verses from other chapters. The Book of Mormon text of Isaiah is not "word for word" the same as the words of Isaiah contained in the King James Version of the Old Testament. "Of the 433 verses of Isaiah in the Nephite record, Joseph Smith modified about 233. Some of the changes were slight, others were radical. However, 199 verses are word for word the same as the old English version."[151]

After Nephi quoted the Isaiah chapters, he editorialized or explained to his brothers what the quoted words meant. At issue was the inability of the rebellious brothers to understand prophetic words. Laman and Lemuel lacked the spirit of *prophecy*, which means "to utter by divine interpretation." When speaking in the name of the Lord, it was expected that the prophetic message would "be of an elevated nature rather than simply phrased in everyday language. Poetry helps the prophetic message to reach beneath surface meanings by adding rhythmic repetitions intended to focus our attention and touch our souls."[152]

1 Nephi 21:15—Does the word *Israel* in scriptural context refer to more than Jacob and his descendants?

The meaning of *Israel* is "one who prevails with God" or "let God prevail." In holy writ, Israel may refer to any of four things: Jacob, whose name was changed to Israel; tribes or the house of Israel; Israel as a land; and believers in Jesus Christ.[153]

> **1 Nephi 21:16—What is the meaning of "I have graven thee upon the palms of my hands"?**

In antiquity, tattooing the palm of the hand "with the symbol of the temple or other sacred emblems, was to show devotion" to God. In this case, it is a reference to Jesus Christ, His Atonement, and His death.[154]

> **1 Nephi 22:31—Is there any evidence that Nephi's closing signature of his first book shows an Egyptian literary style?**

According to Hugh Nibley, "Egyptian literary writings regularly close with the formal *iw-f-pw*, 'Thus it is,' 'and so it is.' It may not be a coincidence that Nephi ends the main section of his book with the phrase, 'And thus it is. Amen'" (1 Ne. 9:6; 1 Ne. 14:30; 1 Ne. 22:31).[155]

THE SECOND BOOK OF NEPHI

> **2 Nephi—Is 2 Nephi principally a doctrinal book containing a record of the prophecies of Lehi, Nephi, and Isaiah, or is it a continuation of a family narrative?**

2 Nephi is referred to as "one of the greatest doctrinal books" in the canon of scripture. It contains a record of the prophecies of Lehi, Nephi, and Isaiah. With the exception of two of its chapters—the first and fifth—2 Nephi has no historical narration. The only book in the Book of Mormon that has "less to say about the people or culture" is the book of Moroni.[156]

> **2 Ne. 1:5–7—The record states that no one will come to the promised land unless brought or directed by the Lord. In what ways has that statement been fulfilled?**

In affirmation of the scriptural statement, Anthony W. Ivins, a member of the First Presidency under President Heber J. Grant, said that "[The Lord] brought the faith of the devoted Puritans of New England; he brought the patriotism of the Dutch at New

York; he brought the gallantry of the cavaliers of Virginia; the light-hearted energy of the French of New Orleans. Just the kind of composite body of men to establish a government that could not be dominated by any particular race or tongue, but made composite, that all men might be welcomed to it, live under and enjoy its privileges."[157]

2 Nephi 1:6—Why are quotation marks missing from such phrases as, "I, Lehi, prophesy"?

There is not even one quotation mark in the entire Book of Mormon, perhaps because ancient Nephite recorders were not familiar with this type of punctuation.[158] What about punctuation in general? The original text of the Book of Mormon as scribed by Oliver Cowdery and others had no punctuation except dashes in the individual book summaries.[159] John H. Gilbert, typesetter of the 1830 Book of Mormon, reported, "Every chapter . . . was one solid paragraph, without a punctuation mark, from beginning to end."[160] It is interesting that the King James Version of the Bible doesn't have quotation marks either.

2 Nephi 1:6—Have scholars made observations about Book of Mormon names or compared Book of Mormon names to the those in the Old Testament?

According to scholars, there is not a name in the Book of Mormon that begins with the letters *F, Q, W, X,* or *Y.* It may not be a coincidence that none of the proper names in the Old Testament begin with these same letters.[161]

2 Nephi 1:14—After Lehi reminds his sons of the Lord's mercy in bringing them out of Jerusalem, he commands them to "Awake! and arise from the dust, and hear the words of a trembling parent, whose limbs ye must soon lay down in the cold and silent grave, from whence no traveler can return." Why do critics suggest that his phrase, "no traveler can return," was taken from Shakespeare?

In an attempt to show that Joseph Smith was not the translator of the Book of Mormon, Book of Mormon critics attribute Father Lehi's words in 2 Nephi 1:14 to William

Shakespeare. (Lehi lived about 2,100 years before Shakespeare was born.) The critics' reference is to *Hamlet*, Act 3, Scene 1, Lines 79–80: "But that the dread of something after death, The undiscovered country from whose bourn no traveller returns." These critics overlook the fact that a similar statement was made by Job. Historian B. H. Roberts suggests that the book of Job could have "furnished the complete thought and even largely the phraseology to both Lehi and Shakespeare."[162] The scriptures in Job say, "Are not my days few? cease then, and let me alone, that I may take comfort a little, Before I go whence I shall not return, even to the land of darkness and the shadow of death. . . . When a few years are come, then I shall go the way whence I shall not return" (Job 10:20–21; Job 16:22).

William Shakespeare

their grasp. For example, Nephi wrote, "I glory in my Jesus, for he hath redeemed my soul from hell" (2 Ne. 33:6). Enos wrote, "I soon go to the place of my rest, which is with my Redeemer; for I know that in him I shall rest" (Enos 1:27). Alma the Elder was told that he would have "eternal life" (Mosiah 26:20).[163]

---

2 Nephi 1:15—How common was it for Lehi to express confidence that "the Lord hath redeemed my soul from hell"?

The Book of Mormon testifies of several prophets besides Father Lehi who expressed confidence that salvation was within

2 Nephi 1:15—Lehi's reference to God having "arms of love" and later references to ears, eyes, face, and loins suggest that God has a body. How many times in the Book of Mormon does it say or imply that God has a body?

Metaphorical interpretations advocated by Philo and Maimonides attempt to make God incorporeal. The Book of Mormon does not advocate such a metaphorical interpretation. The Book of Mormon tells of a living God who possesses a body. References to His having a body occur 283 times in the Book of Mormon, including references before the birth of Jesus (see Ether 3:16). These references show that God's body was used to assist and benefit the ancient Americans. For example, the Lord symbolically used His hands to guide (see 2 Ne. 1:24) and to recover (see 2 Ne. 21:11) His children. The following are Book of Mormon references to God having a body:

Arm	1 Ne. 20:14
Arms	2 Ne. 1:15
Holy Arm	Enos 1:13
Open Arms	Morm. 6:17
Back	2 Ne. 7:6
Blood	Alma 5:21
Bowels	Mosiah 15:9

Ear	2 Ne. 7:5
Ears	2 Ne. 15:9
Eye	Jacob 2:15
All-Searching Eye	2 Ne. 9:44
Eyes	2 Ne. 3:8
Eyes of His Glory	2 Ne. 13:8
Piercing Eye	Jacob 2:10

Jesus Christ with a physical body

Face	2 Ne. 7:6	Pleasant Voice	Hel. 5:46
Feet	3 Ne. 11:15	Small Voice	3 Ne. 11:3
Finger	Alma 10:2	Still Small Voice	1 Ne. 17:45
Flesh	Alma 7:12	Still Voice of Perfect Mildness	Hel. 5:30
Hand	1 Ne. 20:13		
Hands	2 Ne. 1:24	Voice of Thunder	1 Ne. 17:45
Left Hand	Mosiah 5:10		
Palms of My Hands	1 Ne. 21:16		
Right Hand	1 Ne. 20:13		
Lips	2 Ne. 21:4		
Loins	2 Ne. 21:5		
Mouth	2 Ne. 3:21		
Shoulder	2 Ne. 19:6		
Side	3 Ne. 11:14		
Tongue	2 Ne. 7:4		
Voice	1 Ne. 16:25		
Mighty Voice	Alma 5:51		
Mildness of the Voice	Hel. 5:31		

2 Nephi 2:11–16—Why is "opposition in all things" central to the plan of salvation?

Like Jacob (see Gen. 49), Lehi warned and blessed his children. In the blessing to his son Jacob, Lehi gave a discourse on the great plan of salvation, also known as the plan of happiness. Within that divine plan is the concept of "opposition in all things." The central reason for opposition was the need for the Fall of man (see 2 Ne. 2:22–24). By having "opposition in all things," mankind is asked to make a choice between good and evil (see 2 Ne. 2:11).

This concept is central to the plan; as Brigham Young taught, "Evil is with us, it is that influence which tempts to sin, and which has been permitted to come into the world for the express purpose of giving us an opportunity of proving ourselves before God, before Jesus Christ, our Elder Brother, before the holy angels, and before all good men, that we are determined to overcome the evil, and cleave to the good, for the Lord has given us the ability to do so."[164]

Lehi taught his son Jacob that there must be opposition before "man can be truly free and before he can experience real joy." Therefore, the concept of "opposition in all things" includes "1) every law has both a punishment and a blessing attached to it, 2) disobedience to law requires a punishment which results in misery, 3) obedience to law provides a blessing which results in happiness (joy), 4) without law there can be neither punishment nor blessing, neither misery nor happiness—only innocence, 5) thus happiness (or joy) can exist only where the possibility of the opposite (unhappiness or misery) also exists, and 6) in order to exercise free agency a person must have the possibility (and the freedom) of choice."[165]

Brigham Young

2 Nephi 2:21—Repentance is the key to turning from sin in order to embrace the joy of the plan of salvation. What does *repentance* mean?

The word *repent* is found 313 times in the Book of Mormon. It means to turn from sins and imperfections and be cleansed through the blood of Jesus Christ. It also means to turn back or come back to the covenant agreement between God and His children. By repenting, the Nephites returned to the covenants between God and their ancient fathers—Abraham, Isaac, and Jacob.

President Ezra Taft Benson asked the membership of The Church of Jesus Christ of Latter-day Saints to repent: "We have not been using the Book of Mormon as we should. Our homes are not as strong unless we are using it to bring our children to Christ. . . . And our nation will continue to degenerate unless we read and heed the words of the God of this land."[166]

> **2 Nephi 2:28–30—In what ways did keeping the commandments assure the Nephites of safety from the powers of the adversary as the plan of salvation unfolded in their lives?**

The Prophet Joseph Smith taught, "The devil has no power over us only as we permit him. The moment we revolt at anything which comes from God, the devil takes power."[167] Thus, it was important for the Nephites to keep the commandments of God if they were to enjoy the plan of salvation. When they failed to keep the requisite commandments and remember the mercies of God, they became subject to the adversary and did not have joy in the plan of salvation.

> **2 Nephi 3:1–25—As Lehi blesses his son Joseph, he tells of the prophesies of Joseph of Egypt and of another Joseph, like unto the first, who will bring salvation to his people. To whom was Lehi referring?**

2 Nephi 3:1–25 tells of four different men named Joseph— Joseph of Egypt; Joseph, the son of Lehi; Joseph Smith Sr., and Joseph Smith Jr. Joseph Smith Jr. is the Joseph who, like Joseph of Egypt, brought salvation to his people.

In an inspired blessing to his son Joseph, Joseph Smith Sr. said, "Thy father Joseph, the son of Jacob. Behold he looked after his posterity in the last days, when they should be scattered and driven by the Gentiles, and wept before the Lord; he sought diligently to know from whence the son should come who should bring forth the word of the Lord, by which they might be enlightened and brought back to the true fold, and his eyes beheld thee, my son; his heart rejoiced and his soul was satisfied."[168]

Brigham Young said of Joseph Smith, "It was decreed in the counsels of eternity, long before the foundations of the earth were laid, that he, Joseph Smith, should be the man, in the last dispensation of this world, to bring forth the word of God to the people, and receive the fulness of the keys and power of the Priesthood of the Son of God. The Lord had his eyes upon him, and upon his father, and upon his father's father, and upon their progenitors clear back to Abraham, and from Abraham to the flood, from the flood to Enoch, and from Enoch to Adam. He has watched that family and that blood as it has circulated from its fountain to the birth of that man. He was fore-ordained in eternity to preside over this last dispensation."[169]

2 Nephi 3:11—In what ways does a seer differ from a prophet?

Although the words *prophet* and *seer* are often used interchangeably, Ammon speaks of a seer being "greater than a prophet," a prophet having a testimony of Christ (Mosiah 8:13–17; JST, Gen. 50:25–33). Ammon further explains that "a seer is a revelator [one who is authorized to tell what has been seen] and a prophet also; and a

gift which is greater can no man have" (Mosiah 8:1). A seer can see, but it is not ordinary sight: "The seeric gift is a supernatural endowment."[170] A seer can perceive hidden truth. President Ezra Taft Benson taught that a prophet was an inspired teacher whereas a seer foresees the future.[171]

2 Nephi 3:12—Does the phrase "shall grow together" refer to the Bible and the Book of Mormon coming together to convince the world that Jesus is the Christ, or does it mean something else?

Prophets, seers, and revelators in the latter days testify that the Bible and the Book of Mormon convince the world that Jesus is the Christ. Brigham Young said, "The Book of Mormon in no case contradicts the Bible. It has many words like those in the Bible, and as a whole is a strong witness to the Bible. Revelations, when they have passed from God to man, and from man into his written and printed language, cannot be said to be entirely perfect, though they may be as perfect as possible under the circumstances; they are perfect enough to answer the purposes of Heaven at this time."172

Joseph F. Smith said, "[The Book of Mormon] cannot be disproved, for it is true. There is not a word of doctrine, of admonition, of instruction within its lids, but what agrees in sentiment and veracity with those of Christ and His Apostles, as contained in the Bible. Neither is there a word of counsel, of admonition or reproof within its lids, but what is calculated to make a bad man a good man, and a good man a better man, if he will hearken to it. It bears the mark of inspiration from beginning to end, and carries conviction to every honest-hearted soul."173

Heber J. Grant said, "The Book of Mormon is in absolute harmony from start to finish with other sacred scriptures. There is not a doctrine taught in it that does not harmonize with the teachings of Jesus Christ. There is not one single expression in the Book of Mormon that would wound in the slightest degree the sensitiveness of any individual. There is not a thing in it but what is for the benefit and uplift of mankind. It is in every way a true witness for God, and it sustains the Bible and is in harmony with the Bible."174

George Albert Smith said, "These two books [the Book of Mormon and the Bible] hand in hand teach us all where we came from, why we are here, where we may go, and they both contain the advice, the loving advice of our Heavenly Father intended to inspire us to do that which will enrich our lives here and prepare us for eternal happiness."175

Ezra Taft Benson said, "The Book of Mormon is the keystone in our witness of Jesus Christ, who is Himself the cornerstone of everything we do. It bears witness of His reality with power and clarity. Unlike the Bible, which passed through generations of copyists, translators, and corrupt religionists who tampered with the text, the Book of Mormon came from writer to reader in just one inspired step of translation. Therefore, its testimony of the Master is clear, undiluted, and full of power. . . . Truly, this divinely inspired book is a keystone in bearing witness to the world that Jesus is the Christ." 176

According to Elder Boyd K. Packer, Ezekiel's prophesy that the stick of Judah and the stick of Joseph "shall grow together" is fulfilled (Ezek. 37:15–20). Elder Packer said, "[They] are now woven together in such a way that as you pore over one you are drawn to the other; as you learn from one you are enlightened by the other. They are indeed one in our hands. Ezekiel's prophecy now stands fulfilled."[177]

2 Nephi 3:18—Who was the "spokesman" raised up by the Lord?

Sidney Rigdon was the "spokesman" raised up by the Lord to assist Joseph Smith. In the Doctrine and Covenants, Sidney is referred to as "a spokesman to my servant Joseph" (D&C 100:9). Of Sidney, Elder

Sidney Rigdon

George Q. Cannon said, "He was baptized in the town of Kirtland, and the foundation of a great work was laid there. God afterwards revealed that this man was to be a spokesman, and he became the spokesman to this people and to the world for the prophet Joseph. Those who knew Sidney Rigdon, know how wonderfully God inspired him, and with what wonderful eloquence he declared the word of God to the people. He was a mighty man in the hands of God, as a spokesman, as long as the prophet lived, or up to a short time before his death. Thus you see that even this which many might look upon as a small matter, was predicted about 1,700 years before the birth of the Savior, and was quoted by Lehi 600 years before the same event, and about 2,400 years before its fulfillment."[178]

2 Nephi 4:12—Why did Nephi include so little family narration after the death of Lehi?

After the death of his father, Nephi did not continue to write a family narrative. Instead, he wrote doctrines of the kingdom and apparently asked his younger brother Jacob to do likewise (see

2 Ne. 4:15; Jacob 1:1–4).[179] Why the shift? We don't know. 1 Nephi is a family narrative, whereas 2 Nephi is all about doctrine.

2 Nephi 4:16–35—Is Nephi becoming more poetic or self-disclosing as he writes his praise of God?

This passage is often referred to as "the psalm of Nephi." In ancient Israel, psalms were hymns of praise and thanksgiving that were to be read aloud or sung, and were a form of expression used by Nephi and other ancient prophets. Psalms expressed religious feelings at a deep and highly intense or emotional level. Because of these customs, it was perhaps natural for Nephi to "write the things of [his] soul" in poetic form.[180]

2 Nephi 5:5–9—Were the descendants of Nephi the only ones who took upon themselves the name *Nephite?*

The word *Nephite* has various meanings, including all "who are friendly to Nephi" (Jacob 1:13–14), a religious community (see 3 Ne. 2:12–14), and a combination of "ites" (see Jacob 1:13). Therefore, reference to a "Nephite" may not refer to a descendant of Nephi.[181]

2 Nephi 5:15—Nephi writes of iron, copper, brass, and steel and other metals being found in the promised land. What archaeological findings show evidence that ancient Americans worked with precious metals?

Archaeologists have verified the existence of a pre-Columbian monetary system (see Alma 11:4–19), copper (see 1 Ne. 18:25; 2 Ne. 5:15), sophisticated tools (see 1 Ne. 17:9; Jarom 1:8; Ether 10:25–26), machinery (see Jarom 1:8), and excellent highways (see 3 Ne. 6:8). Alloys like steel and brass are not as evident in archaeological findings. Scholars have also found evidence of advanced civilizations, fluctuations in economic growth, trends in migration, and devastations of war. As to the frequency of precious metals being mentioned in the Book of Mormon, iron is mentioned eighteen times, steel five, copper eight, brass thirty-seven, silver fifty, gold sixty, and ziff once.

Scholars long argued that "no real Jew would ever dream of having a temple anywhere but in Jerusalem." Then in 1952 the Brooklyn Aramaic Papyri disclosed that Jews living far from Jerusalem built a temple in their new locale. As the scholarly community was reeling over that news, Hugh Nibley wrote of Jews settling on the Nile at Elephantine and erecting a temple. According to Nibley, when the temple at Elephantine was "destroyed by the hostility of a local governor," Jews living in the area "applied to the directors of the temple at Jerusalem for permission to rebuild it—which permission was granted."[182] The Book of Mormon mentions Nephite temples in the land of Nephi (see 2 Ne. 5:16), Zarahemla (see Mosiah 1:18), and Bountiful (see 3 Ne. 11).

As to temple-building among the Nephites and the Latter-day Saints, LDS Church Historian Andrew Jenson said, "Many of you brethren who are comfortably fixed financially, could, single handed, build a temple like Solomon's temple with your own means. You might be obliged to follow the example of Nephi in not furnishing the building with so much silver and gold or so many precious things as did Solomon, but I venture to say that it was quite possible for a small number of Nephites to erect a temple as large as that erected by Solomon [ninety feet in length and thirty feet in width and height], omitting the costly ornamentations."[183]

There were five epochs of Nephite political history: kingship; judges and governors; anarchy and rule by independent tribes; Messianic dispensation; and war, chaos, and extinction of a nation. In their political history, rule by kings lasted the longest. In each of these epoch periods, wickedness was the great divider that led to contentions and wars.[184]

A *curse* is to be cut off from God's presence (see 2 Ne. 5:20–21; Alma 3:19). The "mark" upon the Lamanites was "a skin of blackness" (see 2 Ne. 5:21; Alma 3:6–13). According to Daniel Ludlow, "This is the only reference in the entire Book of Mormon where a definite color adjective is used to refer to this mark. All other references call it a 'skin of darkness' or a 'dark skin.'" (The words *blackness* and *darkness* are interchangeable in the Hebrew language.)[185]

Elder Milton R. Hunter wrote of seeing variations in skin tones in the Bonampak murals of Mexico and in Indian paintings on the walls of the Temple of the Warriors in Yucatan. Mayan scholars point to similar depictions on Mayan ceramics and other artifacts.[186]

2 Nephi 5:26—What is the location of "the land of my people"?

The First Presidency of the Church and the Quorum of the Twelve have not made a statement as to Nephite geography. In 1890, Elder George Q. Cannon said, "There is a tendency, strongly manifested at the present time among some of the brethren, to study the geography of the Book of Mormon. We have heard of numerous lectures, illustrated by suggestive maps, being delivered on this subject during the

A Frederick Catherwood etching of ruins in Central America

present winter, generally under the auspices of the Improvement Societies and Sunday Schools. We are greatly pleased to notice the increasing interest taken by the Saints in this holy book. . . . The brethren who lecture on the lands of the Nephites or the geography of the Book of Mormon are not united in their conclusions. No two of them, so far as we have learned, are agreed on all points, and in many cases the variations amount to tens of thousands of miles. These differences of views lead to discussion, contention and perplexity; and we believe more confusion is caused by these divergences than good is done by the truths elicited. How is it that there is such a variety of ideas on this subject? Simply because the Book of Mormon is not a geographical primer."[187]

Years later, Donl Peterson wrote, "To superimpose a Nephite map on top of a current map of the western hemisphere is, at best, personal supposition."[188] There is, of course, much information in the Book of Mormon for constructing a relative geography for the Book of Mormon. Scholar John Sorenson and others have paid careful attention to the internal evidence.

2 Nephi 5:26—Did the Book of Mormon ever have geographic and historical footnotes?

The 1897 edition of the Book of Mormon was divided into chapters and verses with footnote references by Elder Orson Pratt. Pratt included geographic locations within the Nephite and Jaredite civilizations. For example, he noted the river Sidon as the Magdalena River in Columbia (see Alma 22:27), the land of Desolation as North America (see Alma 22:31), the land of Bountiful as South America (see Alma 22:31), the Waters of Ripliancum as Lake Ontario (see Ether 15:8), and the narrow neck of land as the Isthmus of Panama (see Alma 22:32). These geographic footnotes, along with historical footnotes, were removed in the 1920 edition of the Book of Mormon.

2 Nephi 5:26—Did Joseph Smith say anything about the location of "the land of my people"?

On January 4, 1833, Joseph Smith wrote to N. C. Saxton, editor of a newspaper in Rochester, New York: "The Book of Mormon is a record of the forefathers of our western Tribes of Indians . . . By it we learn that our western tribes of Indians are descendants from that Joseph that was sold into Egypt, and that the land of America is a promised land unto them." When the editor failed to print the letter in its entirety, Joseph wrote, "The letter which I wrote you for publication I wrote by the commandment of God, and I am quite anxious to have it all laid before the public for it is of importance to them."[189]

In 1834 on the march of Zion's Camp, Joseph said, "The contemplation of the scenery around us produced a peculiar sensation in our bosoms; and subsequently the visions of the past being opened to my understanding by the Spirit of the Almighty, I discovered that the person whose skeleton was before us was a white Lamanite, a large, thick-set man, and a man of God. His name was Zelph. He was a warrior and chieftain under the great prophet Onandagus, who was known from the Hill Cumorah, or eastern sea, to the Rocky Mountains."[190]

2 Nephi 5:26—Were Levites or descendants from Aaron officiating in the priesthood among the Nephites?

President Joseph Fielding Smith wrote, "There were no Levites who accompanied Lehi to the Western Hemisphere. . . . The Nephites officiated by virtue of the Melchizedek Priesthood from the days of Lehi to the days of the appearance of our Savior among them." All through the Book of Mormon we find references to the Nephites officiating by virtue of the high priesthood after the holy order (see Alma 13:1; D&C 107:1–4). "By the power of this priesthood they baptized, confirmed, and ordained. During these years they also observed the law of Moses. They offered sacrifice and performed the duties which in Israel had been assigned to the priests and Levites. They observed in every detail the requirements of the law."[191]

2 Nephi 6—Did Jacob share with the Nephites the "doctrine" or "doctrines" of the kingdom?

In the Book of Mormon, the word *doctrine* appears twenty-four times, always with a singular meaning: The doctrine of Christ

President Joseph F. Smith

is faith, repentance, baptism, and the gift of the Holy Ghost (see 2 Ne. 31:3–21). When the word *doctrine* appears in the plural, it has reference to foolish or false teachings that deny Jesus as the Christ (see 2 Ne. 28:9, 15; Alma 1:16).[192] Jacob shared with the people of Nephi the doctrine of the kingdom.

2 Nephi 6:5—Why would Nephi and Jacob quote extensively from the words of Isaiah?

Out of the sixty-six books in the Bible, Isaiah is the only book with the command to search the words (see 3 Ne.

23:1–2). In searching the words of Isaiah, readers will find that the name *Isaiah* means "Jehovah is salvation" and that Isaiah lived near Jerusalem from 760 to 700 BC. They will also discover that Isaiah taught of Christ and of covenants made between God and Israel. Both Jacob and Nephi quote entire chapters of Isaiah and then give editorial commentary to illustrate the efficacy of Isaiah's prophecies. Jesus also quoted Isaiah about events that had or would be fulfilled (see 3 Ne. 16:17; 3 Ne. 20:11).[193] Of the writings of Isaiah, President Wilford Woodruff said, "Three fourths of [Isaiah's] predictions relate to the establishment of the kingdom of God in the latter days."[194] For these reasons and more, Nephi and his brother Jacob quote extensively from the words of Isaiah.

Before quoting Isaiah, Nephi explained why he quoted his words (see 1 Ne. 19:21)— Isaiah told of the Jews of old, the Nephites, the latter days, and the coming forth of the Book of Mormon. The selected Isaiah chapters coincide with the teachings and exhortations of Nephi. Even the sermon of Jacob, in which Isaiah is quoted, mirrors the teachings of Nephi. Jacob admits that the words of his sermon "are the words which my brother [Nephi] has desired that I should speak unto you" (2 Ne. 6:4). A few scholars view "Jacobian Isaiah" as "largely an extension of Nephi's own thoughts."[195]

It was prophesied that the Lord would set up His standard in the last days. That standard is The Church of Jesus Christ of Latter-day Saints (see D&C 115:3–5), the covenant (see D&C 45:9), and the word of the Lord as contained in the Book of Mormon (see 2 Ne. 29:2). Of the standard, President Marion G. Romney said, "This Church is the standard which Isaiah said the Lord would set up for the people in the latter days. This Church was given to be a light to the world and to be a standard for God's people and for the Gentiles to seek to. This Church is the ensign on the mountain spoken of by the Old Testament prophets. It is the way, the truth, and the life."[196]

"There is no mystery to compare with the mystery of redemption, not even the mystery of creation. Finite minds can no more comprehend how and in what manner Jesus performed his redeeming labors than they can comprehend how matter came into being, or how Gods began to be," said Elder Bruce R. McConkie. "We may not intrude

Example of standards from antiquity

too closely into this scene. It is shrouded in a halo and a mystery into which no footstep may penetrate." [197]

Yet we know that in Gethsemane, Jesus "descended below all things as he prepared himself to rise above them all" (Matt. 26:39). Jesus "suffered the pain of all men, that all men might repent and come unto him" (D&C 18:11). As Isaiah prophesied, "All we like sheep have gone astray; we have turned every one to his own way; and the Lord hath laid on him the iniquity of us all. . . . Surely he hath borne our griefs, and carried our sorrows" (Isa. 53:6, 4).

2 Nephi 9:6–12—What is the nature of "spiritual death"?

Spiritual death refers to a spiritual alienation from God; according to Alma, it occurs when one dies "as to things pertaining unto righteousness" (Alma 12:16). The first spiritual death came when Adam and Eve transgressed the commandments of God. The Atonement of Jesus Christ redeemed mankind from the first spiritual death.

Of this President Joseph F. Smith said, "When Adam, our first parent, partook of the forbidden fruit, transgressed the law of God, and became subject unto Satan, he was banished from the presence of God and was thrust out into outer spiritual darkness. This was the first death. Yet living, he was cast out . . . from the presence of God; communication between the Father and the son cut off. He was absolutely thrust out from the presence of God as was Satan and the hosts that followed him. That was spiritual death. But the Lord said that He would not suffer Adam nor his posterity to come to the temporal death until they should have the means by which they might be redeemed from the first death, which is spiritual. Therefore angels were sent unto Adam, who taught him the Gospel and revealed to him the principle by which he could be redeemed from the first death, and be brought back from banishment and outer darkness into the marvelous light of the Gospel. He was taught faith, repentance and baptism for the remission of sins, in the name of Jesus Christ, who should come in the meridian of time and take away the sin of the world." [198]

2 Nephi 9:33—What is the meaning of the phrase "uncircumcised of heart"?

In the Old Testament, the law of circumcision was the sign of a covenant between Israel and Jehovah (see Gen. 17:10–11). The phrase "uncircumcised of heart" refers to those who fail to keep their covenants. The word *heart* appears in 168 verses in the Book of Mormon. In 53 verses the heart yields itself to God and is made to rejoice because of the purity of its intentions. Rejoicing occurs after a great struggle in which the heart is broken and becomes receptive to God's commandments. Of this process President Joseph Fielding Smith said that those with a broken heart are "willing to abide in all the covenants and the obligations which the Gospel entails."[199]

As to the eventual outcome for Lehi's family, those with uncircumcised hearts knew much of Satan's frequent triumph over the will of man. Phrases such as setting their "heart upon riches" (Mosiah 11:14), "stubbornness" (Alma 32:16), and "wickedness" of heart (Alma 10:6) evidence the continued indulgence of Lehi's descendants in the pleasures of a material world. Those who listened to the testimony of prophets had their hearts "melted" (2 Ne. 23:7), "moved" (2 Ne. 17:2), and experienced "lowliness" (Moro. 7:44) of heart. These feelings were necessary for their hearts to become softened (see 1 Ne. 2:16) or broken (see 2 Ne. 2:7).

2 Nephi 9:41—Is the "keeper of the gate of heaven" Jesus Christ, or is it the ancient Apostle Peter?

The Holy One of Israel, even Jesus Christ, is the "keeper of the gate." He "employeth no servant there" (2 Ne. 9:41). The traditional Christian notion that the ancient Apostle Peter is the keeper of the gate is without gospel foundation.

2 Nephi 9:42—Why are the descendants of Lehi so frequently told to "come down in the depths of humility"?

The Lord's vehicle for entreating the hearts of men is humility. Being humble is in direct opposition to being lifted up, puffed up, or swollen in self-importance. To be humble, the descendants of Lehi literally had to descend into the depths, for "notwithstanding their riches, or their strength, or their prosperity . . . they did humble themselves exceedingly before [God]" (Alma 62:49). The word *humility* occurs thirteen times in the Book of Mormon. Seven references use the phrase "the depths" or "dust" of humility. The word *humble* is found in forty-seven verses. In each of these verses, being humble or possessing humility is a desired characteristic even if it has been forced by poverty.

2 Nephi 9:42—How can humility be maintained?

The humble are able to maintain humility only if they "fast and pray oft, and . . . wax stronger and stronger in their humility, and firmer and firmer in the faith of Christ" (Hel. 3:35). The humble are promised that they will be "visited with fire and with the Holy Ghost, and shall receive a remission of their sins" (3 Ne. 12:2).

2 Nephi 12:2—Does the scriptural passage "the moun-

tain of the Lord's house shall be established in the top of the mountains" refer to the Salt Lake Temple or to a high place in which to communicate with God?

The word *mountain* is used both allegorically and figuratively in the scriptures. Depending on the scriptural reference, *mountain* means a "place of revelation," like a temple or a high place of God (see D&C 57:3). Elder LeGrand Richards viewed the Salt Lake Temple as the prophesied "house of the God of Jacob that our pioneer fathers started to build when they were a thousand miles from transportation, and it took them forty years to build it."[200]

2 Nephi 12:13—Several plants, like cedar, are mentioned in the quoted words of Isaiah. What are the other plants mentioned in the Book of Mormon?

In alphabetical order, plants mentioned in the Book of Mormon are: barley (see Mosiah 7:22), briers (see 2 Ne. 15:6), cedars (see 2 Ne. 12:13), corn (see Mosiah 7:22), figs (see 3 Ne. 14:16), fir (see 2 Ne. 24:8), grapes (see 2 Ne. 15:2), lilies (see 3 Ne. 13:28), neas (see Mosiah 9:9), olives (see 1 Ne. 10:12), sheum (see Mosiah 9:9), sycamores (see 2 Ne. 19:10), thistles (see Mosiah 12:12), and wheat (see Mosiah 9:9).[201]

2 Nephi 19:12–21—What is the meaning of the oft-quoted phrase "his hand is stretched out still"?

The phrase *hand of God* is used as an "agent of judgment" (Job 19:21) and as the "means of deliverance" (Job 5:18).[202] The phrase "his hand is stretched out still" is a reminder that God's loving, watchful care over His

Cedars are among the plants mentioned specifically in the Book of Mormon

children has not ceased and that His "arm of mercy" is extended to all.

2 Nephi 21:14—What is the meaning of "they shall fly upon the shoulders of the Philistines towards the west"?

According to Elder Orson F. Whitney, "[Gentile] steamships, their railroads, their means of rapid transit and communication—these are 'the shoulders of the Philistines,' upon which the children of Ephraim have been and are being brought to the West, to the land of Zion, where the New Jerusalem is to rise, where the pure in heart will assemble, and the necessary preparation be made for the coming of the Lord in his glory."[203]

2 Nephi 25:7–16—In what ways does Nephi reframe the words of Isaiah to fit his knowledge of future events?

With the spirit of prophecy, Nephi retells the major concepts found in the quoted words of Isaiah. For example, Nephi speaks of the restoration of the Jews under King Cyrus of

Persia (see 2 Ne. 25:17–19). He writes of Jesus being rejected by the Jews (see 2 Ne. 25:12) and of His death and Resurrection (see 2 Ne. 25:13). Nephi tells of the second destruction of the Holy City of Jerusalem by the Romans (see 2 Ne. 25:14) and of the scattering of the Jews (see 2 Ne. 25:15). He writes of the Jews' eventual acknowledgement that Jesus is the Messiah (see 2 Ne. 25:16). In his commentary on the Isaiah quotes, Nephi reframes the Isaiah material to fit his knowledge of future events.

2 Nephi 25:14—Was Nephi speaking of the destruction of Jerusalem in AD 70 when he wrote that "Jerusalem shall be destroyed again," or was he speaking of a later destruction of the Holy City?

Nephi is speaking of the destruction of Jerusalem in AD 70, a destruction that is not recorded in the New Testament. The Jewish historian Josephus gives one of the most detailed accounts of the Roman siege: "Now, as soon as the army had no more people to slay or to plunder, because there remained none to be the objects of their fury (for they would not have spared any, had there remained any other work to be done), Caesar gave orders that they should now demolish the entire city and temple."[204] The destruction of the Holy City led to the scattering of the Jewish people throughout the civilized world.

2 Nephi 26:29—How does priestcraft differ from priesthood?

The word *priestcraft* means to "make a craft (business) out of being a priest or a religious leader." Those involved in priestcraft teach popular doctrines instead of the word of God. Those who promote priestcraft seek to "get gain and praise of the world; but they seek not the welfare of Zion" (2 Ne. 26:29).

As to the difference between priestcraft and priesthood, Elder George Q. Cannon said, "There is a difference between priestcraft and Priesthood. Priestcraft builds up itself, it is not authorized of God. Priestcraft oppresses the people; but the Priesthood of God emancipates men and women and makes them free."[205]

Elder Bruce R. McConkie wrote, "Priesthood and priestcraft are two opposites; one is of God, the other of the devil. . . . Apostasy is born of priestcrafts."[206]

> 2 Nephi 27:18—How is the scriptural phrase "Then shall the learned say: I cannot read it" fulfilled in the statements of Professor Charles Anthon to Martin Harris?

Of his visit with Charles Anthon between December 1827 and February 1828, Martin Harris said, "I went to the city of New York, and presented the characters which had been translated, with the translation thereof, to Professor Charles Anthon, a gentleman celebrated for his literary attainments. Professor Anthon stated that the translation was correct. . . . I then showed him those which were not yet translated, and he said that they were Egyptian, Chaldaic, Assyric, and Arabic; and he said they were true characters. He gave me a certificate, certifying to the people of Palmyra that they were true characters, and that the translation of such of them as had been translated was also correct. I took the certificate and put it into my pocket, and was just leaving the house, when Mr. Anthon called me back, and asked me how the young man found out that there were gold plates in the place where he found them. I answered that an angel of God had revealed it unto him. He then said to me, 'Let me see that certificate.' I accordingly took it out of my pocket and gave it to him, when he took it and tore it to pieces, saying, that there was no such thing now as ministering of angels, and that if I would bring the plates to him, he would translate them. I informed him that part of the plates were sealed, and that I was forbidden to bring them. He replied, 'I cannot read a sealed book.'"[207]

Charles Anthon

The "characters" that Martin Harris presented to Dr. Anthon

Charles Anthon wrote of his visit with Martin Harris in an 1834 letter. He said that Martin came to New York City to "obtain the opinion of the learned about the meaning of the paper which he brought with him, and which had been given him as part of the contents of the book, although no translation had been furnished at the time by the young man with the spectacles." In a second letter, Anthon wrote, "Each plate, according to [Harris], was inscribed with unknown characters, and the paper which he handed me, a transcript of one of these pages."[208]

This prophecy of Nephi may have included the religious contention that Joseph Smith found in 1820 in Palmyra, New York. Joseph said of the religious atmosphere in Palmyra, "Great multitudes united themselves to the different religious parties, which created no small stir and division amongst the people, some crying, 'Lo, here!' and others, 'Lo, there!' Some were contending for the Methodist faith, some for the Presbyterian, and some for the Baptist . . . priest contending against priest, and convert against convert; so that all their good feelings one for another, if they ever had any, were entirely lost in a strife of words and a contest about opinions" (JS–H 1:5–6).

2 Nephi 28:3–4—When Nephi prophesied of contention among so-called Christian churches in the latter days, was he speaking of contention in Palmyra in 1820 or of contention in general?

2 Nephi 30:4–7—What blessings are promised the Lamanites in the latter days?

President Spencer W. Kimball said, "The Lamanites must rise in majesty and power. We must look forward to the day when they will be 'white and delightsome' (2 Ne. 30:6), sharing the freedoms and blessings which we enjoy; when they shall have economic security, culture, refinement, and education; when they shall be operating farms and businesses and industries and shall be occupied in the professions and in teaching; when they shall be organized into wards and stakes of Zion, furnishing much of their own leadership; when they shall build and occupy and fill the temples. . . . Brothers and sisters, the florescence of the Lamanites is in our hands."[209]

2 Nephi 31:13–17—What is "baptism of fire and the Holy Ghost"?

Baptism is a complete immersion, whether it is a baptism of water or a baptism of fire and the Holy Ghost (see Moro. 6:4). Fire associated with baptism creates a miraculous cleansing that results in a complete remission of sins. To be baptized by fire and the Holy Ghost is to be sanctified by the Holy Ghost (see D&C 19:31). According to Elder Marion G. Romney, "This baptism of fire and of the Holy Ghost here spoken of by Nephi affects

the great change in the hearts of men. . . . It converts them from carnality to spirituality. It cleanses, heals, and purifies the soul. It is the seal and sign of forgiveness."[210]

THE BOOK OF JACOB

Jacob 1:1—Who was Jacob? How did Jacob merit the role of record-keeper of the small plates?

Jacob, the fifth son of Lehi and Sariah, was born during the days of his father's "tribulation in the wilderness" (2 Ne. 2:1). As a child, Jacob "suffered afflictions and much sorrow, because of the rudeness" of his older brothers Laman and Lemuel (2 Ne. 2:1; 1 Ne. 18:17–19). Although Jacob had before him the poor examples of his elder brothers, Jacob chose to mirror his brother Nephi and live a life of faithful obedience to God (see 2 Ne. 2:2–4). Due to his righteous choices, Jacob heard the voice of the Lord "from time to time" and saw the Redeemer, Jesus Christ (see 2 Ne. 11:2–3). Recognizing the faithfulness of his brother, Nephi consecrated Jacob to be a priest and teacher. (The reference to *priest and teacher* is not the same as the office of priest or the office of teacher; the Nephites held the Melchizedek Priesthood.)[211] Jacob magnified his callings by exhorting the Nephites to righteousness and testifying of Jesus Christ (see 2 Ne. 6–10).[212]

Jacob 1:1—Was Lehi's son Jacob named after Jacob of old?

It is not known why Jacob received his Hebrew name. However, it is known that Jacob, son of Lehi, was a descendant of Jacob, son of Abraham and Rebekah.[213] It is significant that Lehi's oldest children have Egyptian or non-Israelitish names while those born after his prophetic call have Israelitish names.

Jacob 1:9—Was anointing a new king much the same as anointing the sick?

To *anoint* is to pour oil on a recipient's head. Anciently, anointing was reserved for blessing the sick, ordaining kings, and setting apart or ordaining worthy men to sacred offices or positions (see Alma 10:3).[214]

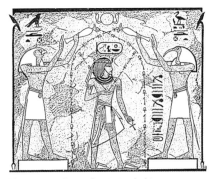

The ancient tradition of anointing the king

Jacob 1:11—Who became the king of the Nephites after the death of Nephi?

First, there is a need to establish that Nephi was a king. From Jacob we learn of a second king being named in honor of Nephi, son of Lehi (see Jacob 1:9, 11). Jacob also tells that under the reign of the second king, the Nephites became wicked (see Jacob 1:15).

The name of the king who succeeded Nephi is unknown. He is referred to only as "Second Nephi," an honorific title given him in remembrance of Nephi. Much of the information about the early Nephite kings was lost due to the loss of the 116 manuscript pages of the book of Lehi. Could Second Nephi have been Jacob? Some scholars support the idea that Jacob was the second king. They claim that

Jacob did not write of his elevated position due to modesty. Other scholars reject the notion that Jacob became king, and suggest that Nephi was succeeded by one of his sons.[215] With this said, the identity of Second Nephi is unknown.

> Jacob 1:13–14—Jacob describes his society as more intricate and complicated than the Nephite society that first broke away from followers of Laman and Lemuel. How many different societies or "ites" were there when Jacob became the record-keeper of the small plates?

Jacob records "now the people which were not Lamanites were Nephites; nevertheless, they were called Nephites, Jacobites, Josephites, Zoramites, Lamanites, Lemuelites, and Ishmaelites" (Jacob 1:13–14). For the purpose of the small plates, Jacob simplified the political situation in which he lived by referring to the "ites" as only Nephites and Lamanites. This same pattern of using the titles Nephites and Lamanites was followed by Mormon and Moroni, who wrote abridged accounts of civi-

lizations in ancient America (see Alma 47:35; Mormon 1:8–9).[216] There were no "ites" during the two-hundred-year period following the visit of Jesus Christ to the ancient Americas.

> Jacob 1:19—Jacob expresses his desire to have "spotless garments." Did he borrow the expression "spotless garments" from ancient origins, or was the expression his own creation?

Several Book of Mormon prophets took off their garments and shook them. By so doing, they signified that they rid themselves of the blood and sins of their generation and magnified their errand before the Lord (see 2 Ne. 9:44; Mosiah 2:28; Morm. 9:35). President John Taylor said, "If you do not magnify your callings, God will hold you responsible for those you might have saved, had you done your duty." Of President Taylor's words, Elder Hugh B. Brown remarked, "This is a challenging statement. . . . If I fail in my assignment as a bishop, a stake president, a mission president, or one of the General Authorities of the Church—if any of us fail to teach, lead, direct, and help

President John Taylor

to save those under our direction and within our jurisdiction, then the Lord will hold us responsible if they are lost as the result of our failure."[217]

Jacob 2—In his temple discourse, Jacob speaks of problems associated with costly apparel, multiple wives, adultery, apostasy, and pride. Why did such ills so quickly dominate his society?

Jacob's people lived in a prosperous, prideful era—an era in which worth was measured by material possessions. Carnal pressures exerted upon the prosperous led to pride. Jacob called his people to repentance in hopes of checking their pride and wickedness.

To acquire material possessions but not take pride in the material goods was challenging for the Nephites; as Elder Bruce R. McConkie said, "The Nephite prophets repeatedly identified the wearing of costly clothing with apostasy and failure to live by gospel standards" (see Jacob 2:13; Alma 1:6; 4 Ne. 1:24; Mormon 8:36–37).[218] Why? Hugh Nibley explained, "Man is always falling away; from Eden to the present moment the human race is in revolt. The chosen people themselves regularly fall from grace and must be called to repentance."[219] The first step in being out of favor with God is pride. When pride is checked, righteousness can prevail.

Jacob 2—It appears that most, if not all, of the ills of life begin with pride. Is there such a thing as "righteous pride," or is there only the "pride" that leads to destruction?

The word *pride* is found in sixty verses in the Book of Mormon; the word *proud* is found in fourteen verses. Of these seventy-four occurrences, not one could be considered righteous pride. Jacob said to the prideful of his day, "[Ye] wear stiff necks and high heads because of the costliness of your apparel, and persecute your brethren because ye suppose that ye are better than they" (Jacob 2:13). President Ezra Taft Benson, quoting C. S. Lewis, reiterated this same thought: "Pride gets no pleasure out of having something, only out of having more of it than the next man."[220]

When pride went unchecked in the Nephite civilization, the ancient people centered their lives on material wealth rather than God. Before long they despised "others, turning their backs upon the needy and the naked and those who were hungry, and those who were athirst, and those who were sick and afflicted" (Alma 4:12). They oppressed "the poor . . . smiting their humble brethren upon the cheek, making a mock of that which was sacred, denying the spirit of prophecy and of revelation" (Hel. 4:12).

> **Jacob 2:35—What type of divine judgment is meted out upon the proud and those who transgress the laws of God?**

The Lord shows forth the following divine judgments in the Book of Mormon:

Anger	1 Ne. 20:9
Angry	1 Ne. 18:10
Fierce Anger	2 Ne. 23:9
Fiery Indignation	Alma 40:14
Fury	2 Ne. 8:20
Chasten	1 Ne. 16:39
Chastened	1 Ne. 16:39
Rebuke	2 Ne. 8:20
Displeasure	2 Ne. 1:22
Jealous	Mosiah 11:22
Sorrows	Mosiah 14:3
Suffer	Mosiah 8:20
Suffereth	Alma 7:13
Sufferings	Mosiah 18:2
Troubled	3 Ne. 17:4
Vengeance	Morm. 5:13
Wept	Jacob 5:41
Wrath	1 Ne. 13:11
Almighty Wrath	Alma 54:6
Cup of the Wrath	Mosiah 3:26

Fulness of His Wrath	1 Ne. 22:17
Fulness of My Wrath	Ether 9:20
Fulness of the Wrath	1 Ne. 22:16

Although the judgmental passions of God are meted out upon the prideful and those who reject the word of God, the Lord showed forth doubly or on a two-to-one basis more loving than judgmental passions in the Book of Mormon. The Lord's attributes of love are recorded 211 times, whereas His judgmental attributes are recorded only 99 times in the Book of Mormon.

Jacob 2–3—In his temple discourse, Jacob appears more sensitive to emotional sways than was his brother Nephi. Is this a correct or incorrect assessment of his character?

In his temple discourse, Jacob describes himself as "weighed down with much . . . anxiety for the welfare of your souls." "It grieveth my soul and causeth me to shrink with shame before the presence of my Maker . . . it burdeneth my soul that I should be constrained . . . to enlarge the wounds of those who are already wounded . . . those who have not been wounded . . . have daggers placed to pierce their souls and wound their delicate minds" (Jacob 2:3, 6, 9). Jacob is the only Book of Mormon recorder to use the words *dread* and *lonesome*. Scholar John S. Tanner writes, "Half the book's references to *anxiety* occur in Jacob, and over two-thirds of the references to *grieve* and *tender* (or their derivatives), as well as *shame*, are Jacob's. He is the only person to have used *delicate, contempt*, and *lonesome*. Likewise, he is the only Book of Mormon author to have employed *wound* in reference to emotions; and he never used it, as everyone else did, to describe a physical injury. Similarly, Jacob used *pierce* or its variants frequently (four of the ten instances in the Book of Mormon), and he used it exclusively in a spiritual sense. Such evidence suggests an author who lived close to his emotions and who knew how to express those emotions."[221]

Jacob 3:1—Jacob comforts the "pure in heart," assuring them that the Lord "will console you

in your afflictions." **In what ways does the Lord console the faithful?**

Although the Lord experienced anguish (see Mosiah 3:7) and grief (see Mosiah 14:10) over the actions of His people, He showed forth the following loving passions in the Book of Mormon:

Comfort	2 Ne. 8:3
Comforted	1 Ne. 21:13
Comfortedest	2 Ne. 22:1
Comforteth	2 Ne. 8:12
Compassion	Mosiah 15:9
Pity	Ether 3:3
Goodness	1 Ne. 1:1
Exceeding Goodness	Alma 60:11
Good	Moro. 7:12
Great Goodness	2 Ne. 4:17
Great Infinite Goodness	Hel. 12:1
Immediate Goodness	Mosiah 25:10
Infinite Goodness	2 Ne. 1:10

A Frederick Catherwood etching of ruins in Central America

Joy	2 Ne. 19:17	Patience	Mosiah 4:6
Pleased	Mosiah 14:10	Long-Suffering	Mosiah 4:11

Pleasure   Jacob 4:9

Rejoice Exceedingly   Jacob 5:60

Love   1 Ne. 11:22

Loved   Hel. 15:3

Loveth   1 Ne. 11:17

Loving Kindness   1 Ne. 19:9

Matchless Bounty
of His Love   Alma 26:15

Mercy   1 Ne. 1:14

Abundant Mercy   Alma 18:41

Exceedingly
Merciful   Jarom 1:3

Great Mercy   Jacob 4:10

Greatness of
the Mercy   2 Ne. 9:19

Infinite Mercy   Mosiah 28:4

Mercies   2 Ne. 1:2

Merciful   1 Ne. 1:14

Multitude of
His Tender Mercies   1 Ne. 8:8

Pure Mercies   Moro. 8:19

Tender Mercies   1 Ne. 1:20

> **Jacob 3:2—In what ways were the passions of God—whether judgmental or loving in nature—predicated upon the actions of the ancient Americans?**

The Lord's passions are not of one hue but a full palette of emotion. His passions, so clearly revealed in the Book of Mormon, appear to be determined by the actions of the Nephites, Lamanites, and Jaredites. When these distinct peoples kept the commandments, gave willing service to others, and set a course toward eternal life, the emotions that God revealed were love (see 1 Ne. 11:22), goodness (see 1 Ne. 1:1), comfort (see 2 Ne. 8:3), patience (see Mosiah 4:6), and mercy (see 1 Ne. 1:14). The strictness with which the people turned their heart, mind, strength, and devotion to God determined the extent and degree of the loving passions they received from Him (see 4 Ne. 1).

During times when the people were not valiant but had not hardened their hearts, the

Lord provided offers of mercy, the blessing of time to repent, and the loving leadership of prophets. When the people flagrantly rebelled against the counsel of God, chose wickedness, and sought to thwart the gospel plan, divine displeasure (see 2 Ne. 1:22), anger (see 1 Ne. 20:9), and wrath (see 1 Ne. 13:11) were evident in God's dealings with them. The degree to which the people were disobedient determined the judgment received (see Alma 36:15). Thus, when the majority rejected God and rebelled against His words, they faced the Lord's fierce anger (see 2 Ne. 23:9) and God's almighty wrath (see Alma 54:6). In the Spirit world, they face His fiery indignation (see Alma 40:14).

Jacob 3:14—Why are the small plates of Nephi referred to as the "plates of Jacob"?

The "plates of Jacob" are the same as the "small plates of Nephi." Jacob wrote on plates "made by the hand of Nephi" (Jacob 3:14). Evidently from Jacob 3:14 on, the plates made by Nephi were called "the plates of Jacob" instead of "the small plates," probably because the recording or inscribing on the plates was now the responsibility of Jacob and his posterity.[222]

Jacob 5—Although Zenos is not mentioned in the Old Testament, he appears to have been a major prophet in antiquity. What is known of Zenos?

Little is known about the personal history of Zenos except that he was a Hebrew prophet who lived before 600 BC and who was slain for testifying of the revelations he had received from God. Zenos had the spirit of prophecy and was quoted on the plates of brass, as shown in the allegory of the olive tree. His prophecies are quoted by Nephi (see 1 Ne. 19:10, 12, 16), Alma (see Alma 33:3, 13, 15), Amulek (see Alma 34:7), Samuel the Lamanite (see Hel. 15:11), and Mormon (see 3 Ne. 10:16). Next to Isaiah, Zenos is the most-quoted prophet in the Book of Mormon.

Jacob 5—In what way is the allegory of the olive tree a representation of Israel?

The allegory or parable of Zenos comprises the longest chapter in the Book of Mormon. "One of the difficulties of the allegory—and of all allegories—is to know how literally it should be interpreted. The dictionary defines an allegory as 'the veiled presentation, in a figurative story, of a meaning metaphorically implied but not expressly stated.' In other words, an allegory is the description of one thing under the image of another."223 With that said, it is presumed that the olive tree represents peace and purity and is an allegorical representation of the house of Israel.

Later, the olive branch signified peace in ancient Greece and Rome. The great seal of the United States features a depiction of an American eagle grasping in its talons an olive branch, a symbol of peace. Thus, the olive branch for centuries has represented peace in various periods of the world.

Of this allegory, President Joseph Fielding Smith wrote, "The parable of Zenos, recorded by Jacob in chapter five of his book, is one of the greatest parables ever recorded. . . . In brief, it records the history of Israel down through the ages, the scattering of the tribes to all parts of the earth; their mingling with, or being grafted in, the wild olive trees, or in other words the mixing of the blood of Israel among the Gentiles."224

Jacob 5—In what way is it evident that Zenos had a correct knowledge of ancient horticultural practices?

According to scholars Paul R. Cheesman and C. Wilfred Griggs, "At no point in the allegory does the author manifest general ignorance on the subject of olive culture. The numerous casual references to pruning, cultivating, fertilizing, grafting, preserving species by grafting, incompatibility, bud sprouts, scion vigor, root rejuvenation, double graftage, root-top growth balances, and invigoration from graftage of wild species are most interesting. . . . In short, this prolonged parable . . . by its accurate incorporation of ancient horticultural practices, invites serious consideration of Joseph Smith's claim that he translated rather than wrote the Book of Mormon."225

Jacob 5:1—Which other prophets also used the allegory of the olive tree in their teachings?

Olive tree

The allegory of the olive tree was used in a fragmentary form in the teachings of Lehi. Nephi refers to his father's teachings of the olive tree by stating, "Yea, even my father spake much concerning the Gentiles, and also concerning the house of Israel, that they should be compared like unto an olive-tree, whose branches should be broken off and should be scattered upon all the face of the earth" (1 Ne. 10:12). The significance of the allegory was not completely understood by Laman and Lemuel, who said to Nephi, "Behold, we cannot understand the words which our father hath spoken concerning the natural branches of the olive-tree, and also concerning the Gentiles" (1 Ne. 15:7). Perhaps one reason for the misunderstanding was that everything in the olive tree allegory is symbolic of something else. For example, the symbols of master, servants, vineyard, trees, and branches represent something of far greater importance. The real significance of the allegory lies in understanding what each symbol represents.[226]

One phrase in the allegory— "it grieveth me that I should

lose this tree"—was repeated eight times. It represents the long-suffering of God. But there comes a time when God's long-suffering ends. Jeremiah compared the covenant people of God to a green olive tree that was consumed by fire (see Jer. 11:16). The Apostle Paul used the olive tree allegory to warn Roman Christians against seeing themselves as being in a more favorable position than the Jews (Rom. 11:16–24).

Jacob 7:1—Who was the first anti-Christ named in the Book of Mormon?

Sherem was the first but certainly not the last anti-Christ mentioned in the Book of Mormon. Nehor (see Alma 1:2–15) and Korihor (see Alma 30:6–60) were also referred to as "anti-Christs." These wicked men "spread their delusions among the Nephites" and led many to embrace their falsehoods and, ultimately, damnation (Jacob 7:2).[227] They taught things that were flattering to the Nephites. They claimed that no one, not even men who claimed to be prophets, could tell the future (see Jacob 7:7) and claimed to have a strong belief in the word of God but admitted

they did not understand His word (see Jacob 7:10–11). They denied the existence of Jesus Christ (Jacob 7:9) and would not accept evidence based on faith (see Jacob 7:13). Anti-Christs counterfeit the gospel of Jesus Christ and the plan of salvation. The ultimate anti-Christ is Lucifer (see Rev. 13:17).

Jacob 7:5, 8—What was the main thrust of Jacob's ministry?

Jacob confronted evil in each vignette of his ministry. Though at times nearly overcome with sorrow by his message of admonition and chastisement, Jacob never shrank from a divine errand. In fact, he spoke with unusual boldness (see Jacob 2:6–10). In his confrontation with Sherem, Jacob was steadfast in his conviction of truth (see Jacob 7:5). Due to his resolute stance, the Lord blessed Jacob with the ability to confound Sherem "in all his words" (Jacob 7:8).

Jacob 7:19—After admitting that he had been deceived by Satan, Sherem feared that he had committed "the unpardonable sin," for he had lied to

Son. What is the unpardonable sin?

In Doctrine and Covenants 76:31–32 the Lord said "concerning all those who know my power, and have been made partakers thereof, and suffered themselves through the power of the devil to be overcome, and to deny the truth and defy my power—they are they who are the sons of perdition," meaning that they have committed the unpardonable sin. Of them Elder Orson Pratt said, "[They] will be banished everlastingly from His presence—body and spirit united together; this is what is called the second death. Why is it called the second death? Because the first is the dissolution of body and spirit, and the second is . . . becoming dead to the things of righteousness."228

Jacob 7:26—In what ways does Jacob's farewell differ from the farewell of his brother Nephi?

Jacob's farewell reveals years of sorrow: "I conclude this record . . . by saying that the time passed away with us, and also our lives passed away like as it were unto us a dream, we being a lonesome and a solemn people, wanderers, cast out from Jerusalem, born in tribulation, in a wilderness, and hated of our brethren, which caused wars and contentions; wherefore, we did mourn out our days" (Jacob 7:26). Yet Jacob, like Moroni, is confident that he will be at the judgment bar (see Jacob 6:13; Moro. 10:27).

In contrast to Jacob's lament, Nephi's farewell reveals self-confidence: "I glory in plainness; I glory in truth; I glory in my Jesus . . . I shall meet many souls spotless at his judgment-seat" (2 Ne. 33:6–7).

Jacob 7:27—As the plates of Jacob passed to Enos and later descendants of Jacob, the spiritual or doctrinal focus of the plates changed from scriptural matters to a genealogical component. Why is there such a genealogy focus in the books of Enos, Jarom, and Omni?

Enos and his descendants wrote more of genealogy than either Nephi or Jacob (see Jarom 1:1; Omni 1:1). These later recorders centered their writings on the history of Jacob's descendants, who probably had little to do with the political or military affairs of the Nephites (see Jacob 1:9). For example, Jarom wrote, "Our kings and our leaders were mighty men in the faith of the Lord; and they taught the people the ways of the Lord" (Jarom 1:7).

THE BOOK OF ENOS

Enos 1:1—What is the origin of the name *Enos?*

The name *Enos* is of Hebrew origin and may mean "man" or "mankind."[229]

Enos 1:1—What was the role of Enos in Nephite society?

Enos and his son Jarom were among "exceedingly many" prophets of their day (see Enos 1:22). Enos described himself as having benefited greatly from the tutelage of his father, Jacob, and was known to prophesy to his people and declare the words of Christ. "I have declared it in all my days," wrote Enos, "and have rejoiced in it above that of the world" (Enos 1:26).

Enos 1:1–27—Is the book of Enos written in a chiastic format or a narrative style?

Chiasmus is a rhetorical device used in prose and poetry to convey a sense of conversion; concepts or ideas are repeated in order to help readers remember what is important. Some chiasms in the Book of Mormon are clear, while others seem vague. Scholar John Welch explains that a chiasmus is a "series of words or ideas in one order, and then repeating it in reverse order . . . the main idea of the passage is placed at the turning point where the second half begins, which emphasizes it."[230] Such literary style or chiastic format is found in the book of Enos and elsewhere in the Book of Mormon; the best example of chiasmus is seen in Alma 36.

Enos 1:3–4–What can be learned from Enos's attempt to communicate with God?

```
idea 4
    idea 3
        idea 2
            idea 1 (important idea
            idea 1   or main point)
        idea 2
    idea 3
idea 4
```

Sample chiasmus structure

The wording used by Enos—"sunk deep," "hungered," "cried," "mighty prayer and supplication," "raise voice high"—indicates that he exerted much personal effort to communicate with God. Enos was so determined to speak with God that he prayed all day and night. "It matters not whether you or I feel like praying," taught Brigham Young, "when the time comes to pray, pray. If we do not feel like it, we should pray till we do. . . . You will find that those who wait till the Spirit bids them pray, will never pray much on this earth."[231]

Enos 1:5–6—What blessings did Enos receive from the Lord?

When Enos placed complete trust in Jesus Christ, repented of his sins, and determined to keep the commandments of God, the Lord spoke peace to his soul. The Lord told Enos, "Thy sins are forgiven thee" (Enos 1:5). Enos accepted the divine forgiveness and was blessed with peace through the atoning power of Jesus Christ (see Mosiah 4:2–3; Alma 36:18–21).

Enos 1:5, 10—The voice of the Lord came into the mind of Enos. What other prophets have had similar experiences?

Many prophetic leaders have received answers to their prayers through the voice of the Lord coming to their mind. One example is President Harold B. Lee, who said, "I was once in a situation where I needed help. The Lord knew I needed help and I was on an important mission. I was awakened in the early hours of the morning as though someone had wakened me to straighten me out on something that I had planned to do in a contrary course, and there was clearly mapped out before me as I lay there that morning, just as surely as though someone had sat on the edge of my bed and told me what to do. Yes, the voice of the Lord comes into our minds and we are directed thereby."[232]

Enos 1:26–27—What is the "more sure word of prophecy"?

Enos was assured through the "more sure word of prophecy" of the rewards of a faithful life (Enos 1:27). Joseph Smith taught that "the more sure word of prophecy means a man's knowing that he is sealed up unto eternal life" or that his calling and election is sure (D&C 131:5).

THE BOOK OF JAROM

Jarom 1:3—How did Jarom express frustration over the wicked practices of the Nephites?

Jarom, like other prophets, used the body as a symbol to express the prevailing conditions of his day, describing his people with phrases such as "hard hearts," "blind minds," "stiff necks," and "deaf ears." Jarom marveled that the Nephites had not been destroyed because of their unbridled sins (see Jarom 1:3), yet recognized their high state of civilization. Jarom described the Nephites as proficient in "fine workmanship of wood, in buildings, and in machinery, and also in iron and copper, and brass and steel" (Jarom 1:8). He also recognized that they had "multiplied exceedingly and spread upon the face of the land, and [become] exceedingly rich in gold, and in silver, and in precious things" (Jarom 1:8). Yet

their actions were not pleasing to God. Jarom learned the long-suffering nature of the Lord God through observing the Nephites' disregard for the commandments.[233]

Jarom 1:5—In what way did Jarom link the word *remembrance* with keeping the covenants of God?

Like other Nephite recorders, Jarom linked remembrance with covenants between God and his chosen people; he and other writers used the phrases "to keep" and "to remember" interchangeably. For example, in Jarom 1:5 the expression is "to keep," whereas in Mosiah 13:16–19 the expression is "to remember" (see Deut. 5:12; Ex. 20: 8).

Jarom 1:11—Why did Jarom not write of publicly teaching and preaching with other prophets of his day?

Although Jarom wrote of "my revelations" and "my prophesying," when he came to writing of "the prophets, and the priests, and the teachers [who] labor diligently, exhorting . . . the people to diligence," he wrote in third person. This suggests that Jarom was not numbered among the prophets, priests, or teachers who labored diligently among the Nephites. Perhaps Jarom was not publicly preaching, or maybe personal modesty prevented him from declaring that he preached with the prophets who "did prick their hearts with the word" (Jarom 1:12).

The Book of Omni

Omni 1:1–12—What makes the Book of Omni unique compared to other books in the Book of Mormon?

The number of record-keepers that inscribed on this one book is unusual. Four of the recorders wrote the first eleven verses of the book of Omni. The fifth recorder wrote nineteen verses. The book of Omni contains fewer than three pages and covers an approximate period of 231 years. Compared with four recorders writing the first five books of the small plates—which covered a period of about 239 years— Omni is not only brief, but is the most unusual book inscribed on the small plates. Then there is the issue of the character of

the recorders. Omni, the first recorder, proclaims that he is a "wicked man," the only Book of Mormon writer to so characterize himself. Amaleki, who cared for the small plates for fifteen years, wrote the most descriptive record in the book of Omni, but it comprises only nineteen verses. Due to the small plates being full, Amaleki made "an end of my speaking" (Omni 1:30).[234]

Omni 1:1–30—What factors may explain the brevity of the book of Omni?

Not only were the small plates full, but the brevity of the book of Omni also suggests apostasy, wickedness, and loss of purpose for engraving on the small plates. To most readers, it appears that the recorders of Omni wrote only a footnote about Nephite history. Scholar John S. Tanner notes, "However pale their own lives must have seemed compared to those of the heroic first generation, however embarrassing it must have been, each man obediently fulfilled his charge, adding his own name to the end of the sacred record."[235]

Omni 1:12–19—Where was Zarahemla located?

On October 1, 1842, the *Times and Seasons* published, "Central America, or Guatimala [sic], is situated north of the Isthmus of Darien and once embraced several hundred miles of territory from north to south.—The city of Zarahemla, burnt at the crucifixion of the Savior, and rebuilt afterwards, stood upon this land."[236] Although this editorial has been credited to Joseph Smith, who was editor of the newspaper at that time, no author is cited.

According to the Book of Mormon, the land of Zarahemla is "down" from the land of Nephi. Daniel Ludlow wrote, "The concept of going 'up' when you go north and of going 'down' when you go south is of relatively recent origin, and thus was not used by the Nephites. When the Nephites stated they went from Nephi down to Zarahemla, they were referring to elevation and not to direction."[237]

The LDS Church has not taken an official position on the location of Zarahemla.

Times and Seasons, Oct. 1, 1842

Omni 1:12–23—Who recorded the account of the reign of King Mosiah I?

The writing of Amaleki, the son of Abinadom, is the only account of the reign of King Mosiah I. It was Amaleki who recorded that during the reign of Mosiah I, the people of Zarahemla were discovered and united with the Nephites (see Omni 1:14–19). Amaleki also told of Coriantumr, the last survivor of what was once a great Jaredite nation (see

Omni 1:20–21). Amaleki gave the small plates to King Benjamin and concluded his record with the poignant call to "come unto Christ" (Omni 1:24–26).

Omni 1:14—Discovery of the people of Zarahemla is the first indication that the Nephites and Lamanites interacted with anyone other than themselves and their descendants. What is the origin of the people of Zarahemla?

The people of Zarahemla descended from those who fled from Jerusalem about 589 BC during the time of Judah's Babylonian captivity (see Omni 1:15). Among those who fled the Holy City was Mulek, a son of King Zedekiah (see Mosiah 25:2; Hel. 8:21). Because only descendants of Judah could rule the kingdom of Judah, it is surmised that Mulek and his posterity descended from the tribe of Judah, but we can't make tribal assumptions about the others who escaped with Mulek.

Although progenitors of the people of Zarahemla left Jerusalem only about eleven or twelve years after Lehi and his family fled the Holy City, a major lan-

Destruction of Jerusalem

guage barrier existed between the Nephites and the people of Zarahemla when they were discovered some four hundred years later. The language of the people of Zarahemla "had become corrupted," for they "had brought no records with them" to the Americas (Omni 1:17).[238]

Omni 1:14–19—What is the meaning of *Zarahemla*?

Stephen Ricks and John Tvedtnes suggest that the proper noun *Zarahemla* is a Hebraic construct meaning "'seed of compassion' or 'child of grace, pity or compassion.'"[239]

Omni 1:25—Why did Amaleki give the small plates—which consisted of six books and the

writings of nine men—to King Benjamin instead of to a king who held the honorific title of Nephi? Had the kingship line moved away from Nephi's descendants?

The fact that King Benjamin ruled over the Nephites seems to suggest that the kingship line had moved away from Nephi's descendants. However, this is not the case. Mormon assures his readers that during the kingship reign of Nephite history "the kingdom had been conferred upon none but those who were descendants of Nephi" (Mosiah 25:13). What *is* apparent in the names of King Mosiah and King Benjamin is that the honorific title of Nephi had been discarded. However, the lineage of Nephite kings remained. When Amaleki, who did not have children, gave the small plates to King Benjamin, Benjamin already had in his possession the large plates of Nephi that contained the secular history of the Nephites.

THE WORDS OF MORMON

Words of Mormon 1:1–18— It is frequently stated that the Words of Mormon were written as a bridge between the small and large plates. What purpose do the Words of Mormon fulfill?

The two pages comprising the Words of Mormon are about five hundred years out of chronological order in the sequencing of the Book of Mormon. The book of Omni ended about 130 BC, and the book of Mosiah begins at 130 BC. The Words of Mormon began in AD 385, near the end of Mormon's life.

Verses one through nine of the Words of Mormon contain editorial comments about Mormon's work with ancient records. The remaining nine verses are viewed as a bridge, providing information about the early years of King Benjamin's reign.

It is interesting that Nephi, who did not understand why he was to make a second set of records (the small plates), defined his confusion by saying, "Which purpose I know not" (1 Ne. 9:5); Mormon, who did not understand why he was to write the Words of Mormon, expressed himself by saying, "I do this for a wise purpose. . . . I do not know all things" (W of M 1:7).

Words of Mormon 1:7—The "wise purpose" must have to do with the loss of the 116-page manuscript. Why is that manuscript referred to as the book of Lehi?

The first edition of the Book of Mormon contained a preface written by Joseph Smith in which he stated that the 116 lost pages contained a translation of the book of Lehi. This means that the book of Lehi contained information spanning from Lehi to King Benjamin.

Words of Mormon 1:7—Was the book of Lehi written on metal plates or on perishable material?

The type of material Lehi wrote on is not mentioned in the Book of Mormon. Some Book of Mormon scholars suggest that Lehi wrote on perishable material such as animal skins (see Jacob 4:12). To confirm their supposition, they point to the Talmud, which specifies that the skins of clean animals be used for writing the law (see Ex. 25:5; Lev. 13:48). Scrolls made from animal skins were also used at the time of Lehi (see Jer. 36:2; Ezek. 2:9–10). To give further credence to Father Lehi writing on perishable material—such as animal skins, papyrus, or clay—there is no mention in 1 Nephi of metal plates being brought by Lehi's family from Jerusalem other than the plates of brass. There is also no mention of smelting ore to create plates until Lehi's family reached the promised land. Then there is the issue of scriptures being burned in a fire and destroyed (see Alma 14:8).

Words of Mormon 1:7— What happened to the 116-page translation of the book of Lehi?

Joseph Smith believed that someone or some persons had stolen the manuscript and that "by stratagem they got them away." Martin Harris did not believe that it was some person or persons; he was convinced that the culprit was his wife, Lucy Harris. Yet without Lucy's immediate confession and no others claiming the deed, speculation has run rampant as to what happened to the manuscript; opinions vary and answers are few. The most definitive answer was received by revelation through Joseph Smith in July 1828—that wicked men had taken and altered the manuscript (see D&C 10:6–8, 10–13).[240]

Words of Mormon 1:7—How did "wicked men" acquire the 116-page manuscript of the book of Lehi?

Martin Harris believed that his wife, Lucy, played a significant role in the acquisition. He believed her capable of the theft. Mother Smith believed, "Mrs. Harris took [the manuscript] from the drawer, with the view of retaining it, until another translation should be given, then, to alter the original translation, for the purpose of showing a discrepancy between them, and thus make the whole appear to be a deception."[241] Palmyra historian Thomas Cook begged to differ. He claimed that Lucy Harris threw the manuscript into a fire and no attempt was made to alter any word of the manuscript. He wrote, "At one time while engaged in a heated argument with her husband [Lucy] grabbed up a bundle of his manuscripts and threw them into the fire."[242]

In later years, Lucy confessed to being a party to the incendiary demise of the manuscript. Her confession, however, is questioned because it was given long after the Book of Mormon was published.

An Abridgment by Mormon

"Wherefore, I, Nephi, did make a record upon the other plates, which gives an account, or which gives a greater account of the wars and contentions and destructions of my people. And this have I done, and commanded my people what they should do after I was gone; and that these plates should be handed down from one generation to another, or from one prophet to another, until further commandments of the Lord." (1 Ne. 19:4)

THE BOOK OF MOSIAH

Mosiah 1—Was Mormon a compiler or abridger of ancient records?

A *compiler* pulls together various documents with an editorial link that makes the documents one. The commonly held view that Mormon was a compiler stems from the fact that there are hundreds of direct quotations in the six condensed books abridged by Mormon—Mosiah, Alma, Helaman, 3 Nephi, 4 Nephi, and Mormon.

An *abridger* is one who rewrites or shortens original accounts. Mormon is an abridger because he condensed the large plates of Nephi into an abridged version on the plates of Mormon. On four separate occasions he recorded in his abridgment, "I cannot write the hundredth part of the things of my people" (see W of M 1:5; Hel. 3:14; 3 Ne. 5:8; 3 Ne. 26:6). Keith Schofield estimates that "64% of [Mormon's] writings are historical, 30% verbatim quotes from the Savior and major Nephite prophets and writers, and 6% doctrinal writings."[243]

In the book of Mosiah, one way to determine which words are Mormon's is to notice that the narration changes from third person to first person when Mormon editorializes. When he returns to third person, he is abridging the ancient record.

Royal Skousen wrote, "Along with the loss of the first 116 pages of the original manuscript which contained the book of Lehi, most of the original first two chapters of the book of Mosiah were also apparently lost. In the printer's manuscript, the beginning of Mosiah was originally designated as chapter III. In addition, the title of the book ('the Book of Mosiah') was later inserted between the lines." Skousen adds, "All other books [within the Book of Mormon] start their account with the person for which the book is named, yet here the book of Mosiah begins with king Benjamin. The original

book undoubtedly began with the account of a Mosiah—Benjamin's father, the first Mosiah. Further, this book is missing the initial book summary that typically begins all the other longer books." 244

The transfer of responsibility for the kingdom from Benjamin to Mosiah included transferring the plates of brass, the Liahona, plates of Nephi, and Laban's sword (see

A Frederick Catherwood etching of ruins in Central America

Mosiah 1:15–16). According to S. Kent Brown, "Custody of these items singled out the possessors as the inheritors of a civilization and heritage established in an earlier age under the direction of the Almighty."245

Mosiah 2:1—What were the Jewish overtones in the coronation ceremony of King Mosiah?

Having the people gather together in families—as if "in pilgrim fashion"—and set their tents facing the temple is similar to festivities associated with the Israelite Festival of Booths and the Passover practice specified in the Talmud.246 The offering of "sacrifice and burnt offerings according to the law of Moses" in the festivities also suggests strong Jewish overtones (Mosiah 2: 3). The fact that the festivities took place near the temple and involved sacred covenants also reveals a Jewish influence in the coronation ceremony.247

Mosiah 2:7—What are the connections between the tower built for King Benjamin and what Joseph Smith called "Tower Hill"?

Joseph Smith identified an ancient site that he called "Tower Hill" located north of Far West, Missouri. Joseph wrote, "[Lyman Wight] lives at the foot of Tower Hill (a name I gave the place in consequence of the remains of an old Nephite altar or tower that stood there)."248 Joseph never suggested that Tower Hill had any connection with the tower built for King Benjamin.

Mosiah 2:9—What impact did King Benjamin's speech have on his people?

King Benjamin's speech—today referred to as "the most widely quoted scriptures in the entire Book of Mormon"—was valued in Nephite society for generations (see Mosiah 8:3; Hel. 5:9). In the speech, Benjamin combined the two great commandments—love God and love your neighbor—into "when ye are in the service of your fellow beings ye are only in the service of your God" (Mosiah 2:17). This important directive is heralded as one of the greatest statements made by man. According to S. Kent Brown, "One might compare the American public's general acquaintance with, and

Abraham Lincoln

esteem for, the Gettysburg Address of Abraham Lincoln" with the esteem in which the discourse of King Benjamin was held by the Nephites. [249]

Mosiah 2:13—Was slavery forbidden among the Nephites during King Benjamin's reign?

"Slavery was forbidden. Nephites, true to their Israelite heritage, could not keep and observe the law of Moses and make slaves of others." [250] In his speech, "Benjamin conveyed strong images of Old World slavery culture by equating service to man with service to God. He explained that in the Old Testament the concept of service means temple service." [251]

Mosiah 4:13–16—What must be done to acquire characteristics of righteousness?

According to King Benjamin, the righteous must cast off the "natural man" and remember the greatness of God and their dependence upon Him, because the natural man—the man of sin—is an enemy to God (see Alma 45:16). The righteous must pray to God daily and be ever steadfast in their faith. By so doing, the Lord will bless them. They will live peaceable lives, fulfill family responsibilities, and succor, or give relief to, the needy (see Mosiah 4:13–16).

Mosiah 2:33—What is meant by "everlasting punishment"?

The Lord revealed to the Prophet Joseph Smith, "the punishment which is given from mine hand is endless punishment, for endless is my name. Wherefore—eternal punishment is God's punishment" (D&C 19:10–11). President Joseph Fielding Smith said, "The laws of God are immutable, and from this explanation we learn that the same punishment always follows the same offense, according to the laws of God who is eternal and endless, hence it is called, *endless punishment* and *eternal punishment* because it is the punishment which God has fixed according to unchangeable law. A man may partake of endless torment, and when he has paid the penalty for his transgression, he is released, but *the punishment remains and awaits the next culprit, and so on forever.*"252

Mosiah 5:7—Why is Jesus referred to as both the Father and the Son in the Book of Mormon? Is this "divine investiture of authority"?

Jesus Christ is referred to as both the Father and the Son in the Book of Mormon (see Mosiah 15:1–4; Ether 3:14). The Father and the Son are titles, not names. The First Presidency and Quorum of the Twelve explained divine investiture of authority as, "In all His dealings with the human family Jesus the Son has represented and yet represents Elohim His Father in power and authority. This is true of Christ in His preexistent, antemortal, or

unembodied state, in the which He was known as Jehovah; also during His embodiment in the flesh; and during His labors as a disembodied spirit in the realm of the dead. . . . Thus the Father placed His name upon the Son; and Jesus Christ spoke and ministered in and through the Father's name and so far as power, authority and Godship are concerned His words and acts were and are those of the Father."253

Mosiah 5:10—What does it mean to "take upon you the name of Christ"?

Elder Dallin H. Oaks said, "Our willingness to take upon us the name of Jesus Christ affirms our commitment to do all that we can to be counted among those whom he will choose to stand at his right hand and be called by his name at the last day. In this sacred sense, our witness that we are willing to take upon us the name of Jesus Christ constitutes our declaration of candidacy for exaltation in the celestial kingdom. Exaltation is eternal life, 'the greatest of all the gifts of God'" (D&C 14:7).254 Elder Neal A. Maxwell said, "When we take upon ourselves [Jesus'] name and covenant to keep His commandments, it is then that we become His sons and daughters, 'the children of Christ.'"[255]

The faithful endurance of the collective faithful is mentioned in the Book of Mormon, but their individual names do not appear. Perhaps one reason for the omission has to do with the purpose of the Book of Mormon, which is to convince "the Jew and Gentile that Jesus is the Christ, the Eternal God" (title page). The purpose of the Book of Mormon is not to list the names of the faithful. This reasoning is consistent with Nephi's stated desire to not encumber the metal plates with genealogies (see 1 Ne. 6).

The single mention of Amaleki in conjunction with the sixteen men sent to the land of Nephi in search of those who had left the main body of the Nephites several years before is very important (see Omni 1:27–30). About nine years later and from other plates, Mormon picks up the story of the group of men who went in search of those who had left years before; he mentions Amaleki going "down into the land of Nephi" (Mosiah 7:6). As John A. Tvedtnes said, "An author may promise in the course of writing to return to a subject later to supply further details. Actually keeping such a promise can prove difficult. Even with modern writing aids, memory can betray a person into failing to tuck in the corners of plot or information. Mormon . . . made these types of promises at least seven times and in each case, including the Amaleki account, he and his son Moroni made good the promises." [256]

Zeniff and those who followed him left Zarahemla in hopes of returning to the land of Nephi during the reign of Mosiah I (see Omni 1:12). In the reign of Mosiah II, Ammon and others were sent to discover the whereabouts of Zeniff's people (see Mosiah 7:1–2). Chronologically, the record of Zeniff extends from about 200 to 121 BC. During this eighty-year period, the people of Zeniff were ruled by Zeniff, Noah, and Limhi. Note: Mosiah 9–10 was taken directly from the record of Zeniff and is written in first person—"I, Zeniff. . . ."[257]

Mosiah 10:6—What pattern did the Lamanites follow in naming their kings?

The tradition of naming kings after their earliest leader appears the same for the Nephites and the Lamanites. In Jacob 1:11, the king succeeding Nephi, the son of Lehi, was known as Second Nephi. Subsequent kings carried the title of Nephi. It appears that the Lamanites followed the same pattern; for example, the son succeeding King Laman was referred to as Laman (see Mosiah 24:3).

Mosiah 10:12–17—What traditions of the Lamanites were passed from generation to generation?

The false traditions of the Lamanites passed from generation to generation. Each tradition stood in direct opposition to the founding history of the Nephite civilization. For example, the Lamanites taught that Laman and Lemuel were "driven out of the land of Jerusalem because of the iniquities of their fathers" (Mosiah 10:12). The Lamanites believed that Laman and Lemuel were "wronged in the wilderness by their brethren, and they were also wronged while crossing the sea" (Mosiah 10:12). They contended that Nephi usurped the right to rule "the people out of their hands," (Mosiah 10:15) and that Nephi was a robber who took from Laman and Lemuel "the records which were engraven on the plates of brass" (Mosiah 10:16). These false traditions and others caused the Lamanites to hate the Nephites for many generations.

Mosiah 11:3—What type of metal is "ziff"?

Ziff is an unknown metal. However, it is likely to be a shiny metal, because the Hebrew word *ziyv* means "brightness" and is a reference to metallic brightness (see Dan. 2:31).[258]

Mosiah 11:20–29—Why did false priests flourish during the reign of King Noah?

In any era corrupt priests are embraced by the wicked, because their words of deception soothe the conscience of evil-doers (see Moses 5:16; Ex. 5:2). Since King Noah was the epitome of an unrighteous king, he had no qualms about surrounding himself with false priests.

Mosiah 12—In what ways were Abinadi's prophecies about the destruction and death of King Noah fulfilled?

Abinadi prophesied that the seed of the priests would suffer, be scattered abroad, and slain (see Mosiah 17:15–18); that prophecy was fulfilled between 90 and 77 BC (Alma 25:7–12). Abinadi also prophesied that King Noah and his people would be hunted by the Lamanites and that the king would die by fire (see Mosiah 17:9–10). In the not-so-distant future, King Noah died by fire and his people were hunted by the Lamanites (see Mosiah 19:20).

Mosiah 13:1–10—Abinadi knew that he would live to deliver his message to King Noah even though circumstances suggested otherwise. Did Joseph Smith also have assurance that he would live to fulfill his mission when persecution and mobocracy pointed to his imminent death?

In 1840 Joseph Smith Sr. told his son Joseph, "'You shall even live to finish your work.' At this Joseph cried out weeping, 'Oh! My father, shall I?' 'Yes,' said his father, 'you shall live to lay out the plan of all the work which God has given you to do. This is my dying blessing upon your head in the name of Jesus.'"[259] Like Abinadi, Joseph Smith lived to fulfill his appointed mission on the earth.

Mosiah 14—Were there multiple copies of the plates of brass?

When Abinadi quoted the words of Isaiah, he did not have access to the plates of brass. The plates of brass were in the custody of King Mosiah, who had received them at his coronation from his father, King Benjamin. Since Abinadi recited the Isaiah text nearly verbatim, it is assumed that he had access to the words of Isaiah that were on the plates of brass. This suggests that copies of the sacred text, in whatever form, must have been available to Abinadi and others.[260]

Mosiah 17:1–4—Alma had been one of the wicked priests of King Noah, but Abinadi's words changed the course of Alma's life. What was the long-term impact of Alma's conversion?

Alma—a descendant of Nephi and one of the priests of King Noah—was converted by Abinadi (see Mosiah 167:2). For about three hundred years, the religious writings of the Nephites centered on Alma and his descendants—his son Alma, his grandson Helaman, his great-grandson Helaman, his second-great-grandson Nephi, and his third-great-grandson Nephi, a disciple of the resurrected Lord. Because Alma hearkened to the words of Abinadi, Alma was able to impact for good the religious course of the Nephites for more than three hundred years.

Mosiah 17:2—What is the origin of the name *Alma?*

The Latin *Alma* is a name given to a woman. The phrase *alma mater* means "foster mother" or "bounteous mother" and is associated with a protective institution like a university. Is Alma also a semitic masculine name? Professor Yigael Yadin found near the northwestern shore of the Dead Sea an ancient land deed bearing the names of those who had leased property under Bari-Kokhba. One of the names was "Alma, son of Yehudah." Professor Yadin's find suggests that *Alma* is a semitic masculine name meaning "youth" or "lad."[261]

Mosiah 17:13–20—Was Abinadi a religious martyr?

Elder Bruce R. McConkie wrote, "In the gospel sense, martyrdom is the voluntary acceptance of death at the hands of wicked men rather than to forsake Christ and his holy gospel."[262] Like

Christ—who endured scourging, mockery, thorns, and death—His prophets endured persecution and afflictions because of their faith in God. Nephi fled from his plotting brothers (see 2 Ne. 5:1–5); Alma and Amulek endured imprisonment (see Alma 14:22); Ether dwelt in the cavity of a rock (see Ether 13:18); and Abinadi suffered death by fire (see Mosiah 17:20). Of those named, Abinadi is the only one considered a religious martyr.

Mosiah 18:1–14—Why did Alma immerse himself while baptizing Helam?

Abinadi

The issue is whether Alma had been previously baptized. The book of Mosiah does not state whether Alma had been baptized before hearing the words of Abinadi. However, President Joseph Fielding Smith wrote, "Alma was baptized and held the priesthood before the coming of Abinadi, but he became involved with other priests under the reign of the wicked King Noah, and when he baptized Helam, he felt he needed a cleansing himself so he buried himself in the water as a token of full repentance."[263] President Smith added, "When Alma baptized himself with Helam that was not a case of Alma baptizing himself, but merely as a token to the Lord of his humility and full repentance."[264] By being immersed in the water with Helam, Alma showed his willingness to be a witness of God.